THE
LOST ART
—— OF ——
LEADERSHIP

MODELING • MENTORING • MULTIPLICATION

DR. JAMES B.
RICHARDS

The Lost Art of Leadership: Modeling, Mentoring and Multiplication

ISBN: 0-924748-59-1

UPC: 88571300029-1

Printed in the United States of America

© 2005 by Dr. James B. Richards

Milestones International Publishers
4410 University Dr., Ste. 113
Huntsville, AL 35816
(256) 536-9402, ext. 234; Fax: (256) 536-4530
www.milestonesintl.com

1 2 3 4 5 6 7 8 9 10 11 / 09 08 07 06 05

CONTENTS

⋘⋙

INTRODUCTION

L eadership is a delicately balanced combination of developing people and accomplishing goals. When the balance is just right, goals are accomplished, teams are built, abundant productivity occurs and a palpable peace ensues throughout the organization. Conversely, the absence of this finely tuned balance gives rise to emotional and professional chaos. A leader who does not develop people is constantly hiring and firing while facing insurmountable frustration with people who seem to never quite measure up! At the same time, a leader who consistently fails to accomplish goals becomes a source of frustration to the organization and usually faces the loss of his or her job.

For years the professional world seemed to hold to an archaic mind-set that subtly conveyed the idea that "people are not important; only production is important." More recently, however, low productivity on the part of disillusioned workers and paranoid middle management with an "I am disposable" complex have forced the world of business to rethink its position. Today it is widely acknowledged that people are not only important but are, in fact, the greatest resource in the workplace. Developing the people of the organization is now the proven path to reaching goals, meeting deadlines and fulfilling dreams.

The Lost Art of Leadership

Great leaders understand that developing people is the ultimate key to productivity with peace. It is the framework from which great companies are built. An investment in the person pays off with every task while investing in the task only pays off one time.

In their best-selling book, *The One Minute Manager*, authors Kenneth H. Blanchard and Spencer Johnson addressed a basic fear in the workplace that generated the faulty logic that has led us into the dark ages of leadership: "If management wins the workers lose. If workers win management loses."[1] It doesn't have to be either-or. There are time-honored leadership principles that guarantee a win-win situation. *The Lost Art of Leadership* shows how to have the best of both worlds: a workplace where everyone can win.

Frustration may be the single greatest enemy of the leader in the 21st century. Whether religious leaders, politicians or corporate heads, all are fighting what seems to be a losing battle against the lack of self-initiative and personal responsibility as well as the generally eroding work ethic that permeates this country today. Leaders who properly identify the problem and incorporate the laws of modeling, mentoring and multiplying overcome the ineptness our society creates. Those who continue in the failing leadership practices of the past simply perpetuate past failures.

To borrow a well-known maxim, "To continue doing the same thing and expecting different results is insanity." We have inherited the experimental, theoretical, archaic concepts of leadership from the generation that brought us to this point of ineffectiveness. Somehow we think we can do what we have always done and get a different result. Trust me, no matter how hard you try, no matter how much you push your people, you will continue to face all the fears and frustrations of ineffective leadership until you incorporate new leadership values that focus on building people.

It is time for us to return to those time-honored concepts that have been proven through millennia of application. This does not mean we will do everything exactly the same way. It simply means we incorporate three immutable values into our approach to leadership: *modeling*, *mentoring* and *multiplication*.

The Lost Art of Leadership introduces and refines these three most important components of developing your team, your staff or your group to accomplish goals and objectives while developing a great team of leaders and workers. Whether you are developing a multi-billion dollar company, a group of volunteers or a religious organization, these time-honored elements, if applied consistently, will help you build an unbeatable leadership team that will ensure the success of your group. The loss of these elements in our society over the years has resulted in billions of dollars in lost revenues, not to mention the immeasurable cost in undeveloped human potential and endless frustration.

You *can* develop your group into a world-class team of low maintenance, high achievers. *The Lost Art of Leadership* will provide you with the principles, the tools and the insight to build a real team. Apply these principles, and you will learn how to experience maximum productivity with minimum frustration.

Endnote

1. Kenneth H. Blanchard and Spencer Johnson, *The One Minute Manager* (New York: Berkley Books, 1983).

Chapter One

LAYING A SOLID
FOUNDATION

A church youth choir gave their choir director a cap as a gag
gift. It was a standard baseball-style cap except that it had
two bills angled about 45 degrees from each other. On the
front of the cap above the bills were the words: "I'm their
leader...which way did they go?"

Tongue-in-cheek? Certainly. Lighthearted? Without a doubt.
Yet, in its humorous way, the cap with its clever caption reflects a
sobering reality of modern society that affects every area of our
lives, whether home, school, church or marketplace: the growing
dearth of true and effective leaders.

Today, more than ever before, people in every discipline and
endeavor are crying out for skilled, principled leaders to help them
succeed. Leaders in every field yearn to be effective at working with
people, yet so many lack the knowledge or the training to do so.
Some leaders find the struggle too challenging and taxing and simply
surrender to a cycle of unbroken frustration and despondency that

cripples their ability to lead and demoralizes those under them. Others, however, keep plugging away, and with determination, fortitude and personal initiative press on to succeed against the odds.

Leadership is fast becoming a lost art in America as well as in the rest of the industrialized world. Who among us can forget the "perp walks" of major corporate executives accused of embezzlement and cheating their companies, investors and shareholders out of millions of dollars? The shadows of Enron and WorldCom loom large on our horizon and are only the tip of the iceberg. And what about the prominent and highly visible religious leaders who tragically have fallen in disgrace in recent years because of moral failure or financial irregularities? Political figures routinely have their moral peccadillos plastered on the front pages of newspapers and newsmagazines and discussed on the media networks.

We watch all of this with a mixture of dismay, disgust and sadness, and we wonder how the lives of these people got so out of control. Those of us who are leaders recognize that with the right turn of events it could have been us—and pray it will never happen.

Leaders do not fall overnight. Men and women of integrity do not simply wake up one morning and decide to destroy their life's work. It happens by degrees: a shortcut here, a compromise there; eventually it all adds up. The world of leadership is a minefield of potential traps that can weaken us personally, sabotage our hopes for the future and even destroy our lives.

Everywhere I look today I see leaders in every field who are yielding either knowingly or unknowingly to those subtle yet deadly tendencies that, at the very least, will frustrate their desires to be good leaders and may even result in the loss of their leadership function.

Something has gone wrong. We need to restore the lost art of leadership. It's time to reexamine our paradigms of leadership and the way we deal with people. The old philosophies and attitudes of the past will not work in our modern 21st-century world. What we need is to return to the *ancient* principles: the time-honored and time-proven principles and philosophies that have been used for centuries by the wisest of men and women to raise up effective leaders.

A Critical Balance

If leaders do not fall overnight, neither are they formed overnight. Leadership does not happen by accident. Effective leadership is the result of careful planning, thorough training and conscious determination and effort. It hinges on understanding and achieving balance between two critical factors: *developing people* and *accomplishing goals*. These two factors are all-important because neglecting either one will upset the balance of the organization and may even cause it to topple. Any organization that fails to develop people neglects its most important resource. At the same time, an organization that fails to accomplish its goals negates its very reason for existing.

The two critical factors: developing people and accomplishing goals.

Developing people and accomplishing goals go hand in hand. What's the purpose of developing people if they have no goals to shoot for? Conversely, how can any organization accomplish goals without trained, developed people to do the work? Proper attention to the development of people virtually guarantees the accomplishment of goals because everyone will then be "on the same page" regarding the organization's philosophy and mission. At the same time, when the balance is in place, the need to accomplish goals will drive and guide the creation of an appropriate plan and process for developing people.

Long gone are the days for businesses and other organizations when the widespread, if unwritten, philosophy was, "Production matters; people don't." People are the greatest asset and the most valuable resource we have, and the organization that neglects the development of its people—in every area— does so at its own peril.

A truth I learned many years ago is that people don't need answers; they need solutions. What's the difference? In a production-driven environment, answers go for the quick-fix; the fly-by-night patch job thrown in place so that nothing interferes with productivity. Problem solved—for the moment. Answers are cosmetic solutions that may work for a while, but unless a permanent fix is found, the same problem will turn up again later more serious than before.

A people-driven environment, on the other hand, always seeks solutions, not just answers. Solutions address the root cause of the problem. Once the cause of the problem has been identified, a solution can be worked out to correct the problem so that it does not keep cropping up. An answer is a bandage to cover the wound; a solution is the antibiotic that destroys the infection.

Build People, Not an Organization

The foundation is the most important part of a house. Without a good foundation, a house will fall. It is not a question of *if* it will fall; it is simply a question of *when* it will fall. Likewise, the effective leader who will endure time and temptation must build an effective foundation for life, family and profession, whether in business, ministry, political office or any other environment that calls for leadership.

The more tumultuous the environment, the more the need for a sure foundation. Today, in every sphere of life, we live in a tumultuous environment as never before. Our computerized, information-saturated age has transformed modern human society more quickly and in ways undreamed of even a couple of generations ago. Thanks to the Internet, the World Wide Web and instantaneous global satellite communication, our world is much smaller than it used to be. Famine in Nigeria, a tsunami in Indonesia, violent insurgencies in Iraq, nuclear brinksmanship in North Korea; all of these and more are brought daily right into our own living rooms. Geography no longer separates us from the problems and turmoil of the world.

The shrinking of the "global society" along with all its storms, pressures, temptations, struggles and battles provide new and unique challenges for leaders in the 21st century. Every organization, whether a business or a service club, whether a church or a synagogue or a mosque, is filled with people who bring with them not only skills and gifts and assets and talents but also fears, uncertainties and life and family issues. Every day leaders everywhere must deal with people who have problems.

> *The ultimate leader builds the organization by building people.*

There was a time when the leadership mantra for business was that employees should leave their problems at home and not bring them onto their jobs. Decades of neglect of workers' personal lives and needs, and the general decline in productivity coupled with the rise in employee absenteeism and turnover it produced, exposed the fallacy of this approach.

Human beings cannot be compartmentalized. We are whole, unified beings, and our job performance is affected by our physical health, our emotional stability and our sense of spiritual and/or aesthetic fulfillment. Wise and effective leaders take all these factors into account and structure the organizational environment to address them.

The leader's job is not limited to building an organization. The ultimate leader builds the organization by building people. To depart from this focus is to depart from the only sure foundation for effective leadership. The entire organization will suffer as a result. Some leaders somehow end up viewing themselves as the commander-in-chief or at least a drill sergeant. "I have a job to do and a responsibility to carry out," they say, "and if these are the people I have to work with, I will use them to get the job done." And that's exactly what they do; they *use* the people.

People who are merely used like commodities do not last long. They become disgruntled, they feel unappreciated and eventually (sooner than later) they become undependable. Resentment and bitterness build up and fuel a spirit of resistance to any new ideas or initiatives or "projects" cooked up by management. This contributes to high rates of absenteeism and turnover.

The leadership mantra for the 21st century is, "Build people, and the organization will grow." People are our most important asset and resource and only by building strong people can we build strong, effective organizations that accomplish their goals in an environment of peace and harmony. As people develop personally to build a strong organization, they share in the success. They also benefit from the process. Everyone wins!

Leadership Flows From Life

Preparation for leadership is the most essential part. How one prepares determines everything else. Your entire future as a leader will be directed by the foundation you establish in preparation. Life is the best preparation for leadership because life is where we establish the mind-set and belief system that will guide (or drive) everything we do. It would be hard to overestimate the importance of the right preparation because the beliefs and thought patterns we develop in our early years are not easily changed.

You may already be in a leadership position. You may already have years of experience hiring and firing, counseling employee problems, evaluating employee performance and managing a diverse staff or workforce. But do you have peace? Are you seeing the results in the people that you want to see? Are your people becoming whole and stable? Are they growing in confidence in their ability to do the work? Are they proving capable of handling greater responsibilities? Are they accomplishing the organization's goals in an atmosphere of harmony, high morale and optimism? Or are they emotionally and functionally crippled codependents who drain the life out of you because they feel incapable of doing anything on their own? Does your organizational environment promote self-confidence and self-initiative or fear and uncertainty?

Are strife, frustration or other negative emotions the order of the day in your group? Is every project hampered by the inefficient work of undependable people? I heard someone say once, "If you don't like the results you're getting, you're going to have to try something you've never tried." If the problems in your organization arise from a faulty belief system on your part, you can retrain yourself, but it won't be easy.

That's why good preparation from the beginning is so important. There is actually no difference in the preparation for life and the preparation for leadership. If we try to separate the two, our leadership principles will be of little value in the practical areas of life. After all, it is in the practical areas where people need the most help. The people we lead are real human beings with real needs and real feelings. They need help in knowing how to raise their families, how to succeed at work and how to get along in an unreasonable world.

Life is the training ground and the only real preparation for leadership. Anybody can learn leadership principles, but only those who have developed the *character* of leadership can apply them effectively. True leadership is a product more of who we *are* than of what we *do*. When what we do is the product of who we are, it flows out of our heart effortlessly. Even years later the words of a respected Christian educator ring in my ears: "The life of the ministry is the life of the minister." The same could be said for leaders in any area. In fact, that statement could be reworded to say, "The life of *leadership* is the life of the *leader*."

Whatever is in your heart will come out in your leadership. For example, the way you treat your family at home is a good indicator of how you will treat your staff or your workers. If you are full of hurt, you will hurt people. If you are full of rejection, you will breed rejection in people. If you are angry, you will make the people angry. Let's face it; sad people do not make others happy. Rejected people do not make others feel loved. If you are cynical and bitter toward life, it will show in your attitude and leadership style. By the same token, if you are at peace with life and with yourself and your identity, peace will characterize your approach to leadership. Even if you are consciously unaware of it, you will lead from the overflow of your own heart.

*True leadership is a product more of who we **are** than of what we **do.***

Leadership works from what I call the "overflow principle." Whatever we are full of will flow out of us onto the people. We may occasionally rise above our subconscious emotions, but for the most part our leadership will be shaped and colored but whatever is working on our heart. Our heart guides our life, whether in ministry, marriage or business.

The overflow principle is why it is essential that a leader be a whole person. There can be no lingering hurt, rejection or low self-worth working in the life of a leader. Effective leadership requires a strong sense of self-worth because without it a would-be leader will always feel threatened and insecure, and no one can lead from that position. A strong and positive sense of self-worth is important also because of the newest leadership paradigm that has caught hold in the corporate world (even though it has been in the church for centuries): *servant leadership.* The most effective leaders are those who lead by serving, not by dominating, and a servant heart and mindset require a positive self-image and sense of self-worth that do not feel threatened by the ability and success of others.

Servant Leadership

The cornerstone of the new leadership philosophy is *servanthood.* At the heart of this paradigm is the awareness that the key to success is not using other people to fulfill our dreams but helping them fulfill theirs. Helping others is the role of a servant and the dream of someone with a servant's heart. Leaders who approach their role with the attitude of serving and helping their people realize their own dreams and aspirations also guarantee the organization's success in meeting its goals. Most people want to be successful and to grow in what they do. Knowing that the leadership is behind them in this desire and prepared to assist them in every way possible will promote in them a high level of cooperation and optimism.

The key to success is helping other people fulfill their dreams.

Unfortunately, the concept of servanthood is totally foreign to the mind-set of many of today's leaders, not only in business but also, sadly, in the church. They may be able to spout off all the latest leadership principles and axioms with the best of them, and even use all the right leadership words, but they have lost their meaning in the glittering, dazzling allure of "success," American-style.

People are not here to serve us. They are here to serve a cause or a purpose. They should be committed to the organization and its philosophy and goals. Every leader wants a high level of commitment but many fear that a commitment to invest in the people means that the organization will lose, resulting in loss of the dream. Commitment, however, cannot be demanded, not even in return for a paycheck (although in any efficient organization, perpetually uncommitted people will soon find themselves either out the door or reassigned). Commitment must be cultivated. It must emerge from a shared purpose and a trust for leadership. It must be given freely or else it is not commitment. Coerced commitment is nothing but a form of slavery. And everyone knows that slaves despise their masters, no matter how kind they may be.

How, then, do good leaders inspire commitment? One way is by example. Leaders inspire commitment by demonstrating commitment to their people and to the philosophy and goals of the organization. Commitment is a by-product of love, trust and emotional stability. It is highly connected to purpose. If people are to give a high level of commitment, they need to know that they are accomplishing their own personal goals as well. Then, people who know they are genuinely cared for are much more likely to give themselves freely and wholeheartedly to the organization and its mission than those who are made to feel they are only a number or a faceless, disposable entity in the crowd.

As a person who has grown both successful businesses and successful churches, I believe in growth, and I believe in success. But these should *always* be the by-products of helping people. The most successful organizations are those that put their people first; that place genuine value on their gifts, skills, experience, intelligence and creativity; that display a sincere interest in them as *persons* rather than as merely cogs in the corporate machine.

It is time for us to re-evaluate the definition of success. Everybody wants to be successful, but in our materialistic, relativistic and postmodern society many people have lost sight of what success really is. Acquisition of wealth and material gain are no longer the keystones of success they once were. More and more people today are becoming disillusioned by the unfulfilled (and unfulfillable) promises of science, high technology and material prosperity to provide a satisfying and fulfilled life. Stephen Covey in his book *Seven Habits of Highly Effective People* talks about the ladder of success, which some people have spent years climbing—only to find at the top that the ladder was leaning against the wrong wall.[1] This disappointment helps explain in part why more and more people in our society are exploring spirituality for answers. Secular society has failed to deliver contentment, leading many to pursue spiritual alternatives.

Servant leaders are sensitive to this spiritual dimension in their people, and their leadership style and the programs and environment of the organization reflect it. Growth is important, but it is not everything. What is the purpose of growth if it does not build people? If growth of the organization destroys people who bring the growth, we perpetuate an endless cycle of turnover and frustration. We sustain the struggle between leaders and workers to determine who will win. People gladly follow leaders who are committed to the workers' personal success.

People who are developed and fulfilled in every dimension of their lives are happier, healthier, more productive and more enthusiastic about the organization's mission. In practical terms this translates into less turnover, less absenteeism, greater efficiency and a more harmonious work environment.

Success involves growth, but growth alone does not necessarily indicate success. Numerical or monetary growth may simply reflect good organization. A "growing" company or church may or may not be effectively meeting the needs of the people, either its own staff or its customers, clients or members. It may, in fact, contribute to their co-dependency and/or dysfunction even as it continues to grow.

A successful organization, on the other hand, grows numerically and/or monetarily while effectively building up its own people and satisfying its customers. Since this can occur in an organization of any size, size alone then, like growth, is not a factor in measuring success. The most successful organizations are those that, regardless of size, put people first. They build their people while building their organization. One is never sacrificed for the other!

Servant leaders expect growth but pursue it by building people along with the organization. We must be committed to serving people. Any organization that grows beyond its ability to serve people is no longer successful. If your goal is to be a good leader, then your goal must also be to be a good servant. Forget everything you think you know about being a leader until you have screened it through the heart of servanthood.

A servant lives not for his own purposes but for the purposes of others. He always places others ahead of himself and is never offended. Tough standards? Absolutely, which is why we have so many mediocre leaders. Many leaders pass up the chance for greatness because they refuse to take on the mantle (and the demands) of servanthood, preferring to stay in the easier and more familiar yet ineffective paradigms of the past.

Jesus of Nazareth, the greatest and most effective leader who ever lived, said, *"Whoever desires to become great among you shall be your servant. And whoever of you desires to be first shall be slave of all"* (Mark 10:43-44). Of all the radical concepts Jesus introduced, this was probably the most radical and the most threatening. It called for a rethinking of our entire authority and leadership structure.

Our Life Philosophy Determines Our Leadership

Every leader has a philosophy of leadership. The word *philosophy* speaks of ideology, beliefs, views, outlooks, positions and convictions from which we make decisions. Our convictions may be based on many different things. One thing is certain, however; whatever it is based on, correct or not, our philosophy of leadership directs everything we do with people.

Many leaders, perhaps most, are unaware that that have a leadership philosophy. It may be unconscious or unarticulated. They may never have written it down or even thought it through, but it is there nonetheless. Our philosophy of leadership is so powerful that it predetermines every decision we make regarding our people and our organization. In a very real way, most of our future decisions are already made, and we don't even know it. They emerge undetected from the philosophies that guide our decision-making.

Our leadership philosophy grows naturally out of our life philosophy, which determines how we view the world around us and our place in it. It also shapes our attitudes toward authority and our interactions with other people. This means that both our philosophy of life and our philosophy of leadership are tied directly to our self-image and sense of self-worth.

Unfortunately, many leaders have been hurt, burned, abused and generally taken advantage of so often that they have developed some rather defensive methods of dealing with people. Over time many of these same leaders convince themselves that the way they feel about people is normal; that people can't be trusted so it's best not to get close to them. This attitude can become so entrenched in the mind—what the New Testament calls a "stronghold"—that it can be extremely difficult to set aside and replace with another paradigm.

Our philosophies of life and leadership are tied directly to our self-image and sense of self-worth.

People must have purpose in life. It is our sense of purpose that drives us and makes life meaningful. Without purpose there is no motivation; no reason for doing anything at all. Proverbs 29:18 says, *"Where there is no revelation* [*vision*, KJV], *the people cast off restraint."* When people lose purpose, they not only lose motivation, but they also lose restraint. If life has no purpose and no meaning, then it doesn't matter what we do or how we live.

I once heard the saying, "The one who influences your life the most is not the person you believe in, but the person who believes in you." No one wants to open his or her life to someone who will criticize and find fault. But everyone will open his or her life to the one who will encourage and strengthen him or her. This is our job as leaders—to cultivate our people, to draw out the very best in them and to build them up and equip them with the skills and confidence not only to do the work of the organization but also to fulfill their own dreams. As we lead our people to greater success, our trust for them grows, and as we convey that trust they open their lives to us even more!

Congruence and Synchronicity

The way we manage our organization is ultimately an extension of our personal life philosophy. It is essential that there be congruence in the life philosophies, business philosophy and leadership philosophies of ourselves and our team. By "congruence" I mean consistency of purpose, action and intention wherein all parts work together for the same goals. Lack of congruence sends a mixed message to those whom we desire to serve, whether the customer or the congregation.

Congruence makes it essential that all members of the team embrace the same philosophies as the leader. Otherwise, there will be inconsistency in the way people are treated. This inconsistency is sometimes more destructive than a consistently negative philosophy. People want to know what to expect. They do not want to think very much. They want things to be predictable. Inconsistency among the team or anywhere in the organization will result in an inconsistent message and treatment of people.

The goal of congruence is to reach among all members of the team and the organization a *shared vision* or *synchronicity*. Synchronicity is the "seemingly coincidental" order of events that are meaningfully related. In other words, all the people on the team start to think and act in a way that synchronizes every effort. Everything falls together to work for everybody's good.

Servant leadership is absolutely essential for synchronicity because such harmony of activity cannot be achieved through intellectual agreement alone; it requires also a meeting of *hearts*. The heart is where passion and commitment to the vision are unleashed. With synchronicity, the hearts of all team members and all leadership staff begin, as it were, to beat as one. People in intellectual agreement can buy into the mission of the organization, but it takes synchronicity to capture the vision. A synchronous team under the power of a shared vision can accomplish anything.

Think of a formation of geese migrating south for the winter. Few sights are more awe-inspiring than to watch a V-formation of geese in flight, heading in the same direction, aiming for the same goal, wings beating in unison, honking intermittently to encourage each other. The bird flying "point" has the most tiresome position because it breaks the airflow for the rest of the group. At periodic intervals the leader will fall back to a rear position and another bird will assume the "point." If any bird in the formation becomes ill or is injured and has to drop out, at least one of the others will drop out also and stay with it. They won't abandon one of their own.

This is synchronicity in action.

The synchronicity of a shared vision gets everyone "on the same page" regarding the purpose, philosophy and goals of the organization. This common vision in turn helps define the mission—how the organization will accomplish the vision. The principle of servant leadership, which also promotes a servant heart in every member of the team, serves to set the human relations parameters within which the organization must accomplish the vision and live the mission. Each of these can be codified in written form by preparing and publishing the organization's vision statement, mission statement and human relations statement. This way everyone—including customers or clients or anyone else from outside—can understand the purpose and philosophy of the organization.

> *A synchronous team under the power of a shared vision can accomplish anything.*

Identifying our life philosophy is a critical prerequisite to achieving synchronicity. What do we value in life? What is important to us? We can ask ourselves, "If today was my funeral and people were walking by my casket, what would I want my family and friends to say about me?" I have personally redefined this several times over the years. At this point, I would want my family and friends to say, "Jim always made me feel loved, and he always made me believe that God loved me." That is my life vision. What's yours? As a leader I want to influence people in a way that causes them to believe they can accomplish anything!

Once we have identified our life vision, we must consider our ways. We must ask ourselves, "Am I managing my life and relationships in a way that will accomplish this life vision?" At this point it is helpful to develop our own personal mission statement and philosophy of human relations. Next comes the most challenging question: "Is all of this congruent? Will the way I manage my personal life serve my life philosophy and my personal vision and mission?"

The quantum leap comes once we have determined whether our philosophy statements for business and/or ministry are consistent with our life philosophy. Everything we believe must permeate every area of our life, or it causes deep, internal stress and conflict. Until we resolve these issues, we have no hope of building a leadership team that has congruence, much less synchronicity. We cannot lead others until we know where we are going in our personal life as well as in our ministry or business.

As leaders we should want our life, ministry and business to be surrounded by people whose goals and philosophies are consistent with ours. These people will have different strengths and weaknesses; they will do things differently and see things from a different perspective. But they will be guided internally by the same principles that guide our lives. Too many times we staff our leadership team with those who give lip service to our business or ministry philosophies, yet their lifestyle is in total contradiction. A person will always revert back to true lifestyle beliefs, especially under pressure. In such a situation, synchronicity is impossible. Not to mention the flow of inconsistent messages we send to the people we serve.

Our life philosophy will always rule over our business/ministry philosophies. Regardless of our verbal commitment and lofty ideas, apart from a healthy life philosophy we will not be effective leaders. Synchronicity will be an elusive dream.

Win-Win Situations

Those who find the secret to serving the needs of humanity are the ones who find true success. They are the ones who contribute to the quality of life of others. In church, business and life, we are either a giver or a taker. It is in this very issue that our personal philosophies are revealed.

Often we ignorantly embrace a dichotomy about life issues. We think that in every relationship there will always be one who wins and one who loses. It seems impossible that both can win. One of us *must* lose. It is this incorrect rationale that justifies our mistreatment of others. It is this concept that justifies a company's abuse of employees and allows a salesperson to exaggerate to the harm of the customer. It is this paradigm that justifies an organization in using people for its own purpose.

A good deal is good only when everyone wins. When two people want the same thing, both may not get everything each wants, but no one has to lose. A leadership philosophy based on the principle of servanthood, committed to the balance between developing people and accomplishing goals, and focused on achieving synchronicity is the key to building an organization that consistently produces win-win situations for everyone involved. Everybody benefits: leadership, workforce and customers.

The critical key to a life and leadership philosophy of servanthood is the development of a healthy and positive self-identity and sense of self-worth.

Endnote

1. Stephen R. Covey, *The Seven Habits of Highly Effective People: Restoring the Character Ethic* (New York: Simon & Schuster, 1989), p. 235.

Chapter Two

THE IMPORTANCE
OF SELF-IDENTITY

❦

A rthur Miller's Pulitzer Prize-winning play *Death of a Salesman* tells the sad and tragic tale of Willy Loman, a modern-day "everyman" who, in the fading days of his career as a traveling salesman, realizes he has failed not only in his chosen profession but also as a husband and father. In Willy's eyes his two grown sons, Happy and Biff, are failures just as he is. In the final scene, bitter and broken by his shattered dreams and personal failures, Willy kills himself. One of his sons pronounces Willy's epitaph with the words, "He never knew who he was."

What could be more tragic than to come to the end of our days only to discover that our life has been a failure; that we pursued the wrong goals and sought the wrong things because we never knew who we were? Lack of self-identity is a major problem for people in a modern society like ours where truth and morality are relative. With no absolute values or standards upon which to anchor their lives, is it any wonder that so many people who attend our churches or work for our companies have no clear idea at all who they are?

Such lack of identity is tragic in any case, but it is disastrous in a leader. Without clear self-identity we will have no idea where we are going, much less how to get there. With no internal roadmap our pursuits are based on external theories. Consistent plans and predictable accomplishment of goals become impossible. Under such circumstances, no development or duplication of people can occur either. How can a "leader" who has no sense of self model or mentor?

Strong, healthy self-identity lies at the core of effective leadership, particularly servant leadership, because only a leader who knows who he or she is and is comfortable with that identity can lead with confidence, secure and unthreatened by the thought of the success of others.

There is a biblical proverb that says, *"Keep and guard your heart with all vigilance and above all that you guard, for out of it flow the springs of life"* (Proverbs 4:23 AMP). In the context of this proverb the word *springs* means "barriers" or "boundaries." Barriers are the limits we set in our life. All of us have heard the saying, "The sky is the limit." When it comes to personal potential, that phrase is more than just a popular truism. Our success in life as leaders or in any other arena is directly related to the barriers or limits that we set around ourselves.

All of our personal limitations are based on our self-perception. We will achieve only those things that are consistent with our self-perception. The ability to believe we can achieve is a reflection of our sense of self. Therefore, the stronger and healthier our self-perception, the higher we will raise the bar for personal achievement. The better we know ourselves, the more realistically we can see where we are going and the fewer limitations we will place on our ability to get there. And because we know who we are, challenges do not become limitations. Difficulties do not become boundaries.

This means that all our goals are merely extensions of ourselves. If you're a good athlete and believe you have the potential to be a *great* athlete, you will set your sights and goals accordingly: the

Olympics, perhaps, or going professional. If you believe that level of achievement is beyond you (whether it really is or not), you will aim a little lower: teaching or playing for fun in amateur leagues or perhaps coaching children or young people. It all depends on your self-perception, which forges your personal assessment of your capabilities.

> *Strong, healthy self-identity lies at the core of effective leadership*

Our accomplishments will rarely rise above our self-perception. And when they do, we will soon self-destruct to realign our perception and our experience. At the same time, the development of personal skills should rise to the level of our self-perception. A healthy self-perception should be maintained by the character and diligence of personal development. People who constantly try to rise above the true limits of their ability will be constantly frustrated. In time they will diminish their self-worth. Hope deferred makes the heart sick. Failure destroys a heart of confidence, unless character inspires us to overcome the failure.

All of us should seek to stretch and challenge ourselves to go beyond what we *think* we can do because many times we underestimate our potential. In general, setting our sights too low is a much greater problem for us than setting them too high. Most people seriously underestimate their own potential and so go through life unsatisfied and unfulfilled and often don't even know why. The same is true for many leaders.

Here's the bottom line: Our success or failure as leaders or in any other area of life depends on our self-perception; on how we see ourselves, our capabilities, our strengths and our weaknesses. Our self-identity will determine how we view, define and interpret success and how we approach life.

Success or Failure—It's All About You

There are basically three kinds of people, identified by how their self-identity defines their lives.

Some people are driven to *perform* in an effort to bolster an insecure self-identity. These folks believe that success means always moving up to the bigger and the better: bigger house, bigger paycheck, better car, better neighborhood. Their approach to life is performance-driven. They derive their self-identity from what they do and how much they do rather than from who they are. Many workaholics fall into this category. Unless they are constantly exceeding and bettering their past performance they feel worthless, useless and disposable.

Certainly there is nothing wrong with trying to improve all the time and performing better today than yesterday, but that motivation should flow from who we *are*, not from a drive to conform to some false standard of performance. Working constantly to perform better in hopes of shoring up a starved, unstable sense of self-identity is unhealthy and ultimately doomed to failure. We are human *beings* not human *doings*; our self-identity must be based on who we are, not on what we do.

Secondly, there are some people who are driven to *fail* to *confirm* a negative self-identity. These are the folks who have been beaten down so often by failure or told so many times what a loser they are that everything they do enforces a self-perpetuating cycle of failure and inadequacy. They believe they are worthless, and that belief permeates everything they do. They become their own worst enemy. Either consciously or subconsciously they find a way to sabotage every job or benefit or advantage or opportunity that comes their way, thus confirming the negative self-identity. Success in anything lies beyond their grasp (at least in their minds, and that's where it really counts), and they resign themselves to mediocrity, at best. Failure becomes the most distinctive identifying characteristic of their lives.

Finally, there are the well-adjusted people who live successfully as a *reflection* of their self-identity. These are the people who are comfortable in their own skin, at peace with who they are and secure in the love of God, family and friends. Because they have a clear sense of who they are and where they are going, they don't obsess with performance as a means of self-validation. Neither do they feel threatened or insecure by the talents and success of those around them, whether co-workers or subordinates. Life—and leadership—flow from the rich well of being that nourishes their soul, not from some outside source. This richness of being saturates the way they think and work and live so that everything they do and say reflects who they really are.

The Challenge of Identity

The greatest personal battle any of us have to fight in life is the battle for our identity. All other battles revolve around this one. Every day we live we are bombarded by philosophies, ideas and viewpoints on life and living that try to capture our hearts and minds. Myriad voices from every corner of society vie for our attention, seeking to pull us in one direction or another. That is why it is so important for us as individuals and as leaders to be inner-directed by a solid, secure and confident sense of self-identity. The rudder of knowing clearly who we are will help us stay the course against opposing currents as we pursue our dreams, fulfill our potential and lead others in such a way that they can do the same.

Remaining true to ourselves and our vision of life is not the easiest of all paths we could take because along the way lie traps and distractions that could waylay us or even stop us dead in our tracks. The temptation to compromise our values and principles or to seek an easier and more convenient road to success is a constant danger we must watch out for. Living consistently with our self-identity will be the product of a life of vigilance. Only to the degree that we can be undermined in this area can we be defeated. Thus the cause for the admonition, *Guard your heart!*

Two examples from the Bible will be instructive here.

The first is the classic story in Genesis of how Adam and Eve succumbed to the temptation of the devil and lost their identity. According to Genesis, God created man in His own image, which means man (both male and female) was created to be like God.

This was mankind's essential identity. Chapter 3 of Genesis describes how the tempter appeared and immediately challenged the human couple at the very point of their identity.

Now the serpent [tempter] *was more cunning than any beast of the field which the LORD God had made. And he said to the woman, "Has God indeed said, 'You shall not eat of every tree of the garden'?" And the woman said to the serpent, "We may eat the fruit of the trees of the garden; but of the fruit of the tree which is in the midst of the garden, God has said, 'You shall not eat it, nor shall you touch it, lest you die.'" Then the serpent said to the woman, "You will not surely die. For God knows that in the day you eat of it your eyes will be opened, and you will be like God, knowing good and evil." So when the woman saw that the tree was good for food, that it was pleasant to the eyes, and a tree desirable to make one wise, she took of its fruit and ate. She also gave to her husband with her, and he ate* (Genesis 3:1-6).

Look at the tempter's strategy: He starts by planting in Eve's mind questions about God's honesty and forthrightness. He implies that God is holding out on her. Then he attacks at the point of her identity by suggesting that if she eats the fruit of the forbidden tree in violation of God's command, her eyes will be opened and she will *become* like God. He promises her a quicker and easier road to get where she wants to be. But here's the catch: She was already like God. The tempter offered her a cheap (and false) way to get something she already had.

In the end, Adam and Eve both gave in to the temptation and ended up losing their identity. They lost sight of who they were, lost their relationship with God, lost paradise and passed on to all their descendants the pain and confusion of life with a lost identity.

The second example involves Jesus, whom the New Testament refers to as the "second Adam." According to the gospel accounts, just before Jesus embarked on His public ministry He spent 40 days fasting in the wilderness, during which time He was tempted by the devil. As with Adam and Eve in the Garden of Eden, the tempter attacked Jesus at the point of His self-identity.

> *Now when the tempter came to Him, he said, "If You are the Son of God, command that these stones become bread." But He answered and said, "It is written, 'Man shall not live by bread alone, but by every word that proceeds from the mouth of God.'" Then the devil took Him up into the holy city, set Him on the pinnacle of the temple, and said to Him, "If You are the Son of God, throw Yourself down. For it is written: 'He shall give His angels charge over you,' and, 'In their hands they shall bear you up, lest you dash your foot against a stone.'" Jesus said to him, "It is written again, 'You shall not tempt the LORD your God.'" Again, the devil took Him up on an exceedingly high mountain, and showed Him all the kingdoms of the world and their glory. And he said to Him, "All these things I will give You if You will fall down and worship me." Then Jesus said to him, "Away with you, Satan! For it is written, 'You shall worship the LORD your God, and Him only you shall serve.'" Then the devil left Him, and behold, angels came and ministered to Him* (Matthew 4:3-11).

> *The greatest personal battle any of us have to fight in life is the battle for our identity.*

Notice how the entire basis of Jesus' temptation centered around His identity. Twice the tempter said, *"If You are the Son of God..."* and once, *"If You will fall down and worship me...."* In each case the tempter presented Jesus with a quicker, less-demanding route to His goal of being the Savior of His people.

Had Jesus accepted the tempter's offers He would have denied His identity as the Son of God and the Savior of the world. Instead, unlike Adam, Jesus knew clearly who He was and stayed true to His identity by refuting the tempter's offers at every point. Because of this, Jesus successfully accomplished His goal and completed His mission. The first Adam fell because he was confused about his identity; the second Adam conquered because He knew His identity.

The sharp contrast between Adam and Jesus illustrates the importance for all of us of being clear about our identity and remaining true to that identity at all times. Our self-identity includes not only our understanding of who we are as a person but also our personal spiritual, moral and ethical beliefs and values. Temptations are present at every turn to entice us to sell out or compromise our beliefs or values in return (hopefully) for a quicker and easier road to success.

There are no shortcuts to success. There is no substitute for integrity. Nothing can take the place of leading from the overflow of a mature, well-grounded self-identity. Whenever we try to lead in a manner contrary to our self-identity or values, we forfeit our moral authority to lead and send confusing mixed signals to those who are trying to follow us. As leaders, we must first of all learn to be true to ourselves, and to do that we have to know who we really are.

We must avoid the trap of determining our identity by our performance or by any other predetermined criteria. Each of us as leaders must face this challenge in our own particular way. All of us have some standard of success in our minds; some barometer by which we measure how successful we are. If our self-identity is not clearly defined, we will seek that identity in things, in performance or in other people. This will cause us to slip into the mode of *self-fulfilling leadership*—leadership that is designed to meet our emotional needs instead of the needs of the people and the long-term goals of the organization.

For myself, I have found that the soundest base for my self-identity is grounded in a personal relationship with God through faith in Jesus Christ. As far as I am concerned, there is no better way for us to know ourselves or to be prepared for life and leadership than to be in relationship with the One who created us and who knows us better than we know ourselves.

A Solid Self-Identity Provides Stability

A well-grounded self-identity provides stability for our lives in much the same way a solid foundation provides stability for a building. In life, real stability is determined by how rooted and grounded we are in love. The Bible says that God is love (see 1 John 4:16). Since stability precedes power, we should make it our goal to be stabilized by the love of God. Then we will have the power of God to guide us as leaders.

Leaders cannot be reactive; we must be proactive.

When I think of being stabilized, I think of a buoy that floats in the water. No matter how large or powerful the waves, the buoy always returns to the upright position. Why? Because it has a foundation, and its foundation gives it the stability to recover. It is only when we are rooted and grounded in love—love of God, love of family, love of life—that we will have the solid foundation of a secure self-identity that will provide the stability we need in order to be effective leaders.

We live in a reactionary society where we tend to act too late on the wrong information, failing to accomplish the desired results. Leaders cannot be reactive; we must be proactive. Proverbs 22:3 says, *"A prudent man foresees evil and hides himself, but the simple pass on and are punished."* How we respond to situations, not just emergencies but also, and more importantly, the everyday circumstances that arise, must be the product of who we are, which is defined by our sense of identity. Every leader must have a spiritual/emotional anchor that keeps him or her stable in the most troubled waters.

An unstable leader judges events in a subjective manner. He (or she, but we'll use he for now) assumes that everything is about him. His reactions are more about preserving his image than accomplishing the goals. Therefore, he fails to see the larger picture. He creates chaos where there was none. He turns small problems into big ones. The book of Proverbs also says that *"the wicked flee when no one pursues, but the righteous are as bold as a lion"* (28:1). The bold leader does not need to prove or defend his position. He observes life with a clear mind unmarred by a faulty sense of self!

Because he views life in a more objective manner he is able to foresee the unfolding of events, interpret them properly and act accordingly. He knows when to "run" and he knows when to stand. He knows how to seek the proper protection (action). The simple (or unstable) leader is always in chaos. He fails to foresee and plan his strategies. He is like a man who waits until he is thirsty to dig the well.

The prudent leader, on the other hand, foresees opportunities. By staying alert to the currents and the signs around him he is able to forecast the trends in his business or community or church and seize the opportunity to turn those trends effectively to the benefit of his people, the organization and himself. He is not bound either by outmoded traditions or mind-sets or by his own identity limitations. Because he is secure in who he is and what he is after, his need for approval does not dictate his actions.

The power of foresight is found in a peaceful nature. A proactive leader develops the ability to respond calmly to every situation. He is not driven to extremes by uncontrollable emotions and impulses. Instead, he foresees and prepares to "cash in" on the opportunities that less alert and less visionary leaders will miss.

A Stable Self-Identity Eliminates the "Control Syndrome"

Control is probably the single most destructive force today, whether in the church, the office or the boardroom. Leaders who have an unstable self-identity have an innate need for other people to depend on them, to need them and to follow them, thus affirming a self-worth they haven't found in a more healthy source. "Controlling" leadership does not set people free; it makes them more dependent. No organization can run smoothly or efficiently if every item, every decision and every procedure must be micro-managed by an insecure leader. Synchronicity is impossible in such an environment because the purpose of everyone there, rather than to pursue a shared vision, is to serve the leader's demands. Unwittingly, a controlling leader succeeds only in breeding into the people of his team the very attitudes and mind-set that are bringing about his own personal demise. Yet, his faltering ego always strives to remain in control.

Proverbs 28:16 says, *"A ruler who lacks understanding is a great oppressor, but he who hates covetousness will prolong his days."* Power in the hands of an insecure man is as destructive as power in the hands of a wicked man. The wicked and the insecure both lack understanding. Therefore, their methods of oversight will often be very similar, usually resulting in oppression.

> *The greatest oppression today comes from insecure leadership.*

Oppression is another word for force or control. The greatest oppression today, whether in the church or in business, comes from insecure leadership. While a leader should obviously have the final responsibility in decision-making and administration, he should never be in control of the people. People who do not choose to work the plan do not need to be on our team. If we have to force them to work the plan, productivity is lost while dissension and strife increase. Through control we corrupt the organization, the team and our own heart!

Consciously or not, insecure leaders seek to control people because they see control as the only way to secure their own position. Unsure of their own status, unstable leaders fear workers or staff who show creativity or initiative because they view them as a threat. Consequently, these leaders typically either shoot down those creative or innovative ideas or find ways to appropriate them for themselves and take the credit, thereby bolstering their own ego.

Regardless of how you package it, control is control and a controller is an oppressor. If we control people, we may get their labor and their time and their effort, but we will never get their heart. They will never buy into the corporate vision and will have little motivation to do anything beyond the minimum required of them. That's when their work degenerates into nothing more than pursuing a paycheck. When we relinquish control of the people, we may have less to work with but we also will have a lot less trouble. A smaller, more passionate workforce is far more productive than a large group of people who have to be controlled. If they have to be controlled, send them on their way.

Domination by any means creates havoc, discord, strife and everything else contrary to peace and joy and a harmonious work environment. The Bible says, *"For where envy and self-seeking exist, confusion and every evil thing are there"* (James 3:16). The word *envy* speaks of selfish ambition. Selfish and ambitious people are always willing to use other people to fulfill their own goals. No matter how right those goals may be in and of themselves, they become evil when achieving them comes at the cost of violating the dignity and self-worth of other people, who become mere commodities to be consumed in realizing the selfish demands of a dominating and ambitious leader.

Proverbs 28:16 above speaks of hating *"covetousness."* In this context, covetousness speaks of the taking of pillage or spoils from someone who has been conquered. Controlling leaders tend to conquer people, make them surrender their personal vision for that of the leader, spoil them and take their resources. Under this kind of "leadership," staff and workers become little more than indentured servants. The leader who hates covetousness will be an encourager, always helping others to fulfill their own vision and reach their own potential instead of pillaging them to fulfill his or her own.

Allowing the people this freedom instills them with purpose, motivation and commitment—all the things we as leaders desire to see in them. Deprive them of those things, however, and all we will have left is *"confusion and every evil thing."*

Who's Your Hero?

Our source of identity determines our self-image, the way we see ourselves. Our self-image, consequently, determines our behavior, or the way we treat others. Everything is linked, and it all goes back to that point of self-identity. All of us, either consciously or subconsciously, have modeled our self-identity on someone. Because we are human *beings* and not human *things*— because we are *persons* with free will and self-determination and not pre-programmed automatons—we base our own self-identity on a person close to us who we love, admire or respect.

Essentially, the model for our self-identity is the answer to the question, "Who's your hero?" For example, most young boys growing up want to be like their dad. Dad is their hero, their role model. He is the primary source for their developing sense of identity. Likewise, many girls pattern their identity and behavior after their mothers.

The model that shapes our self-identity is the model we will present to other people.

This desire to be like one's parents is perfectly natural in children. For the most part, the self-identity we form in childhood, based usually on a parental model, is the same one we carry into adulthood. It drives the way we look at the world, the way we live our life and the way we interact with people. It also determines and drives our leadership philosophy and style.

As our self-identity takes shape, we begin to take on the image, beliefs, thought patterns and behavior of our identity role model, whoever it is. This means that as we grow we change to become like the person we have adopted as our model.

As I said earlier, I believe the soundest base for our self-identity is found in a relationship with God. In other words, God becomes our identity role model and the measuring stick by which we define ourselves. Whoever our model is, we will behave in a manner consistent with the way our model views the world and the way we view our model.

Take God as our model, for example. If we see God as a strict legalist who demands perfect performance before giving love and acceptance, that's the way we will become. If we believe in a fault-finding God, we will become a faultfinding person and leader. If we view God as a manipulator who uses people only for His own ends, we will become manipulators as well. If we know God as One who operates through personal relationships, we also will become relationship-oriented. If we believe in a God who gives unconditional love and acceptance to undeserving people, we will do likewise.

Whether God or someone else, the model that shapes our self-identity is the model we will present to other people. That is why it is so important to make sure that we have based our self-identity on a worthy model. Although it is not impossible to change the self-identity we formed in our childhood, it is usually quite difficult. It won't happen by accident. Only by careful, deliberate choice and disciplined effort can we replace one model with another one.

Self-Identity Determines Self-Worth

Ultimately, our self-identity determines our self-worth. After we have changed to become like the one we look to for our identity, we then tend to define our worth by the value that person places on us. Thus, our sense of self-worth is determined by the degree to which we feel loved, valued and accepted. The reason we conform to the image of the one who gives us identity is for the purpose of approval. We then base our self-worth on the degree of approval, love and acceptance we receive from that person.

Many performance-driven leaders, for example, try by their constant striving to satisfy an unfulfilled hunger for acceptance by the person or persons from whom they seek respect and acceptance. Their low sense of self-worth drives them to seek approval through performance because they have never found a basis for it within themselves. Many high achievers are driven by the feelings of rejection instilled by perfectionist parents. They seek the approval they never found in healthy relationships.

Self-worth established in the love of God is the deepest realized need of a human being. Freud falsely assumed that sex was the deepest need. Some believe that survival is the deepest need. But history clearly reveals that a human being will sacrifice anything for a genuine sense of self-worth.

Throughout history, millions of people have died to "save face." Billions more have *lied* to save face. Without exception, every moral or ethical problem we face as individuals has its roots in self-centeredness, which is fed by our sense of self-worth. Leaders possessing a strong and healthy sense of self-worth do not use, abuse, manipulate, lie to or hurt people. Instead, they are free to serve and build up people with the self-confidence of servant leaders.

> *Self-worth is the deepest realized need of a human being.*

Self-worth is essential for living a fulfilled life. Our level of self-worth determines how we handle every area of life, whether public or private, at home, at work, at church or wherever. Our level of joy, peace and personal fulfillment will never rise above our level of self-worth. Every abiding positive or negative emotion in life is rooted in our self-worth.

Our self-worth also will determine the heart of our leadership and effectiveness in working with people. The way we treat others and the level of respect and kindness we show are direct reflections of how we feel about ourselves. If our self-worth is nourished by internal sources such as the secure knowledge that we are loved and accepted or by a personal relationship with God, we won't be bothered or obsessed with externals such as performance as a measure of personal value. We won't be obsessed with wondering (or fearing) what other people think of us. Such a view frees us to serve others and to put their needs and dreams and hopes ahead of our own. Not only can we set others free to pursue their dreams and fulfill their potential, but we also can serve them joyfully as they do.

Leaders who have an immature or incomplete or insufficient sense of self-worth inevitably will use others to build it up. Such an attempt is doomed to failure, exacerbating the need for a healthy sense of self. Rather than being servants, such leaders become tyrants, manipulators who simply use people as a means to their own ends. Insecurity is a very poor base from which to lead. Even sound leadership principles will be perverted when operated through insecurity.

Self-worth *must* begin with healthy identity, self-image and self-worth. Self-worth that is not based on identity will be based on performance, accomplishments or some other external and subjective factor. Any so-called self-worth generated by such external factors will be temporary, self-gratifying and ultimately negative and destructive. When our self-worth is tied to our performance (or the performance of others), then it will rise and fall along with that performance. When performance is up, we are up; when performance is down, we're down. That's no way to run a business, operate a church or lead people. And it's certainly no way to live!

Servant leadership in love from a sound base of identity in relationship is the best platform from which to approach leadership. Love always looks to the needs of the other person and tries to meet those needs. Love is self-sacrificial, a concept all but lost in our modern culture. Only the person whose personal worth is intact can consistently walk in love. When self-worth falters, the instincts of self-preservation and self-gratification will always reassert themselves at the expense of service and sensitivity to others. Remember, an insecure person will sacrifice *anything*— including the welfare of others—in order to satisfy his or her own personal need for approval.

Our worth becomes a slave to our standard of success because that standard derives from our identity. Tragically, too many leaders in every arena have accepted a totally false standard of success. They have exchanged true success based on internal values and principles for carnal external standards based on the subjective and ever-changing approval or disapproval of men.

Only when our identity, self-image and self-worth are derived totally independent of performance or results can we be trusted to lead people. Only when we *have* worth can we *build* worth. With our self-worth intact, we will have no hidden, subconscious, egocentric motives. Life will have meaning and purpose, and we will find success and effectiveness because all facets of our life and character will be "in sync." We won't have to worry about having Willy Loman's epitaph over our lives: "He never knew who he was." Instead, we will have a deep, well-grounded sense of identity and personality that will motivate us to reach for our dreams while helping others reach for theirs and propel us toward greatness!

Chapter Three

THE EIGHT CRITICAL
FACTORS OF SUCCESS

⬦

T. S. Eliot once said, "Success is relative. It is what we can make of the mess we have made of things." Although he may have been speaking facetiously, he nevertheless cut right to the heart of one of the primary problems with leadership today. Everywhere we turn we see frustrated leaders who because of inadequate training, poor planning, faulty execution, nonexistent follow-up or any of the above, end up having to make the best of a mess.

The goal of leadership is not a mess but success. No leader sets out deliberately to fail. Failure demoralizes not only the leader but also the team or staff he or she is trying to lead. Why then do so many leaders consistently finish with less than satisfying results? Part of the reason may be that they do not understand success. They may not really know what success is and therefore have no idea how to measure success or how to know when success has been achieved. One thing is certain, however; they will know when it has *not* been achieved. Even if they know what success is, they still may not know how to translate that knowledge into practical results.

They may understand success yet not know how to achieve it. Nothing is more frustrating than to have a vision or to see a dream out in front of you and not know how to get there.

Some people think that great leadership comes naturally, that people are either born leaders or they are not. I disagree.

Great leaders are not born; they are developed.

Not everyone we work with will prove to have leadership potential; that much is true. Even good workers do not always make good leaders. Those individuals who do possess leadership potential, however, can be taught and can become effective leaders as long as they are willing to pay the price in diligence, hard work and consistent application. Through development, mediocre leaders can become good leaders and good leaders can become great. Why stop there? Even mediocre leaders can become great leaders if they possess the willingness to learn and to work and the passion to succeed. All it takes is *understanding* and *applying* the *critical* factors of success.

There are many factors that contribute to success. But it is the *critical* factors that ensure success. In every area of life, success is not about doing *everything* right—no one can do that—but about doing the *critical* things right. As long as we learn the critical factors and do them, we can still succeed even if we don't do everything else perfectly. The person (male or female) who strives to do everything right will only torment himself and those associated with him. He will fail to accomplish his goals and vision and end up angry and bitter and knotted up in a little ball, blaming the world for his failure. If the perfectionist leader reaches what he has labeled as success, he usually arrives on that illusive shore alone. His need to make everything right has left no room for the rest of imperfect humanity in his world.

It's just like in marriage: You don't have to get *everything* right, but there are a few essentials that you *must* get right or else you're in big trouble. The most important thing a leader can do is to find out the most important thing and do it!

As I said, success is not about doing everything right but about doing the critical things right. I want to share with you *eight critical factors for success* as a leader. These are the factors that we use in all departments and at all levels of my church and ministry. They are time-tested and proven effective. Every step is important, so don't ignore or bypass any. Omitting *any* of these steps increases the certainty of frustration and the probability of failure. It also will lower productivity.

The most important thing a leader can do is to find out the most important thing and do it!

If any of these steps are dropped or ignored, your frustration level and that of your team will rise—that is *certain*. Just as certain is the fact that with every step bypassed, failure becomes a higher and higher probability. This is true in any area of life, not just the ministry or the business world.

Not only is every step essential for success, but so is *applying* the steps. Simply knowing them is not enough. Studies have shown that only ten percent of all the people who attend training seminars, whether in ministry or in business or anywhere else, ever actually try to put into practice what they learn. More often they leave saying, "That will never work," or "I could never do that," or "My people would never go for that," or even, "He's got to be kidding," or "I'll put that in practice as soon as I get everything in place."

Well, they're right.

Nothing ever works simply because we *know* it. Putting what we know into *practice* is what makes it work. Dr. Wernher von Braun *knew* how to build a rocket, but if he had never applied that knowledge, the Saturn V would never have been built and Apollo 11 would never have gone to the moon.

I regard these eight factors of success as so critical, and I believe in them so much, that in our ministry, following them is not a suggestion but a requirement for anyone who serves as a leader on any of our teams. I tell all of our leaders, "If you accept a role as a leader in this ministry, you have also accepted the procedures that we follow. The Eight Critical Factors are the eight steps that must be implemented in the role of every leader and in every project. Take it upon yourself to follow these steps when working with others and to apply them when answering to others."

This is critically important because you can't function with a multiplicity of different philosophies at work. Everybody must be working the same plan if success is to become a reality. Working the same plan means that everyone on the team or in the organization accepts and applies the same philosophies, procedures and methods. Unless everyone is on the same page, following the same procedures with the same goals in mind, the result will be confusion, frustration, wasted effort and failure. Success will remain an elusive dream.

Here at Impact we have found the use of a Project Planner to be very helpful for leaders in implementing each step. The Project Planner lays out each of the eight steps in detail. Our leaders, particularly the new ones, use the Planner every time they meet with their team. It helps systematize the approach at first to help make sure that all the steps are followed so that success is a virtual certainty. Eventually, as the leaders gain experience, they can dispense with the Planner, but they still follow the exact same procedure; they have simply internalized it.

In order for these eight critical factors to work, leaders must be proactive in applying them. Don't take them lightly or assume that others understand their importance. Also, do not automatically assume that the steps are being followed. One of the functions of a leader is to provide guidance and to make sure that team members feel safe with what they're doing and how their role fits in with everybody else. That happens under the positive tutelage of a caring, diligent leader.

Here are the eight critical factors of success: *vision, plan, organize, staff, manage, delegate, measure* and *report*. Not only are each of these eight steps critical to success, but they also must be followed in the order given. Each step depends on the successful completion of the preceding one. That is another reason no step should be omitted. To do so will cause a break in the process and every subsequent step will suffer as a result.

Let's now examine in detail each of the eight critical factors of success.

1. Vision

Vision is the starting place for all success. The ancient Hebrew word for vision as found in the Old Testament usually means to have a clear mental picture, although it may sometimes have a more esoteric meaning as well.

When the Old Testament says, *"Where there is no vision, the people perish"* (Proverbs 29:18a KJV), it is talking about a clear mental picture. Every project, every organization must begin from a clear mental picture. We've got to know what we hope to achieve, what the destination is. This is the purpose that keeps everyone motivated and on track.

> *Vision is the first characteristic that sets great leaders apart.*

The vision is the motivator for your team. This is the place we take them mentally when they are demotivated. This is the picture we draw to inspire them.

Vision is the first characteristic that sets great leaders apart from the rest of the crowd. They can see in their heart where they are going and they know what they intend to accomplish.

But great leaders then follow the biblical admonition to put the vision in writing. *"Then the LORD answered me and said: 'Write the vision and make it plain on tablets, that he may run who reads it'"* (Habakkuk 2:2). Many excited people see a vision but can't articulate it. Therefore, they cannot inspire others to run with it. Great leaders have pondered the vision—the end result—to the point where they can draw out every detail.

Great leaders know that the vision has to be clear, understandable and attainable if it is to motivate others. Without vision to motivate, there is only money or force. The vision is written in a vision statement. Everyone knows the target and the destination. As such, everyone becomes a part of keeping the project and even the leader on course.

Mature leaders know that a vision alone is not enough. A vision must turn into a plan or any attempt to fulfill it will result in chaos. It is not enough to know the destination. We must create a map that shows how to reach our destination.

2. Plan

Every vision must be turned into a plan. A plan helps us understand what we intend to accomplish. An important part of any plan is identifying concrete goals to reach as well as the specific procedures to be used in reaching them. Planning also helps identify needed resources, available resources and the means of acquiring whatever is needed. Thorough planning is a must for success.

Planning puts practical elements in place to flesh out the vision. Vision must come before planning because we have to know where we are going if we hope to establish a workable plan for getting there. How can we make plans and set goals if we don't know our destination? If we want to be successful we must be able to see the end *at* the beginning and work toward that end *from* the beginning. Otherwise we will not succeed in reaching our goals even if we're doing good things the whole time. "Good" things become "bad" if they do not advance us toward the goal. Proper planning eliminates counterproductive activities and helps ensure that everyone on the team fully understands and is committed to the vision and the goals for getting there.

The wilderness experience of the ancient nation of Israel provides a good illustration of the consequences of a failed vision. After Moses led the Israelites out of slavery in Egypt and across the Red Sea, they spent 40 years in the desert on what should have been an 11-day journey to the Promised Land. Why? Because they were never fully committed to the goal that God gave them. The

Bible is very clear that their lack of belief kept them from fulfilling the vision. And the Israelites said it was the way they saw themselves that kept them from acting on the plan. Listen to the way the children of Israel viewed God's plan, in light of their self-perception.

> ..."*The land through which we have gone as spies is a land that devours its inhabitants, and all the people whom we saw in it are men of great stature. There we saw the giants (the descendants of Anak came from the giants); and we were like grasshoppers in our own sight, and so we were in their sight*" (Numbers 13:32-33).

Proverbs 29:18 (KJV) says, "*Where there is no vision, the people perish: but he that keepeth the law, happy is he.*" This was certainly true in Israel's case. The entire generation of Israelites that lost their vision of the Promised Land perished in the desert. It was their children and grandchildren who went in and claimed the promise. The second part of the verse says that those who keep the "*law*" are happy. In the sense of leadership and success that we are thinking about here, "keeping the law" means following the plan. In other words, "*he that keepeth the law* [sticks to the plan], *happy* [successful] *is he.*" A good plan helps us keep the vision clearly before us.

Thorough planning is a must for success.

Two excellent tools in the planning process are the *vision statement* and the *mission statement*. The vision statement defines the target. It describes how we will know when we have gotten there. The mission statement is based on the vision statement and says what we are going to do. It lays out the process and procedure for realizing the vision. These two statements give us the nucleus around which the plan evolves.

Once these statements are in place, the next step in the planning stage is to establish specific goals and procedures designed to make the vision a reality.

Preparing a list of questions is always helpful in assessing strengths, weaknesses, assets, needs, etc. For example, here are some of the questions we might want to consider when making the plan:

1. What do we want to accomplish?

2. What is our time frame?

3. What is our budget?

4. What resources do we need?

5. What resources do we have?

6. How are we going to get the resources we don't have?

7. What departments will we use?

8. Who will we get to head up those departments?

Let me give a simple example. Suppose your organization is holding a fund-raiser—a simple carnival, let's say—and one group decides to sell cotton candy. When that group sits down to plan this event, they will have to answer a lot of questions: How many people do we plan to serve? How and where will we get a cotton candy machine? Who will operate the machine? How many people will we need to run the event? What supplies will we need and in what quantities? Who will be responsible for securing those supplies? What will be required for setup and cleanup? A plan makes sure that all these different areas are addressed.

Once we have a plan in place that establishes goals, assesses strengths and weaknesses and identifies all the elements necessary for success, we are ready to proceed to the next step: *organize*.

3. Organize

The word *organize* means to arrange, put in order, systemize, sort out, classify and (this one's my favorite) to bring into being. Proper organization brings the plan into being and the vision into reality. It's like framing up a house from the drawings (the plan). This is the first step to making the plan materialize. Until we organize, our plan is just a dream. I'm sure we've all heard the old truism, "Plan your work and work your plan." Establishing a plan takes care of the first part of that statement; organizing takes care of the second.

It's truly amazing how something so simple is so often overlooked or ignored. Some people never plan. Others plan poorly. Still others may have great plans but never carry them out. The one thing all three of these groups likely share in common is *failure*. Successful people are the ones who move beyond the plan to action. The first action is to organize, to put the parts together in a way that makes sense. Great leaders recognize that even the best plans are valuable only to the degree that they are put into practice. Organizing around the plan helps make this happen.

Proper organization brings the plan into being and the vision into reality.

Proverbs 17:24 says, *"Wisdom is in the sight of him who has understanding, but the eyes of a fool are on the ends of the earth."* In other words, the wise are those who understand where they are going and how they plan to get there while foolish dreamers have no plan at all and therefore look to *"the ends of the earth"* for a solution. This scripture reminds me of those people who are always looking for the "big score," like winning the lottery, or that "one big sale" that will solve all their problems. They are the get-rich-quick schemers who believe that success is merely a matter of finding the right deal or the right formula or being in the right place at the right time.

I once asked a multi-millionaire acquaintance of mine to share 20 t o 30 "tips" that others could use to duplicate his success. Specifically, I asked him about the "breaks" he got or the special deal that helped him turn the corner. As I expected, he denied that anything like that took place. He said, "Jim, there were no big breaks, no one big deal. I just worked hard every day."

Lots of people want to be millionaires; the question is, are they getting up and working hard every day? That's the secret: hard work. There is no such thing as "instant success." Even people who are described as "overnight successes" worked for years to get where they are. Their apparent sudden success was merely the fruit of many quiet, often obscure years of working hard for their goal.

Working hard by itself is not enough. The key is to work hard *on a plan.* This only happens when you organize. You can work hard every day of your life and never go anywhere because your "work" is not coordinated to your goal—if you have one. Having a solid plan is the first step; organizing to work that plan is the second.

Organizing happens by bringing all the pieces of the plan together in a congruent manner. In so doing you identify the various departments and resources necessary and how they must relate to make the project a success. Remember, congruence is when everything and everybody works together toward a common goal with each person fully understanding his or her role, function and responsibility in the overall plan.

I said earlier that in planning it is important to know the end at the beginning. Many times, of course, it is impossible at the beginning to know absolutely everything about the end. There are too many variables to make it certain. To be organized means to know the end *as much as possible* before you start. Organizing helps eliminate many of the variables and unknowns.

One of the most common problems at the organizing phase comes with the assessment of resources. Rarely at the beginning of a project will a team have absolutely everything they need or think they will need. Even with the best planning, all projects evolve in the outworking due to variables and unknowns or unexpected developments and simply because of the dynamic nature of human projects with human involvement. Lack of some of the necessary resources often causes leaders to go to one of two extremes:

1. "I don't have everything I need, so I can't start."

2. "I don't have everything I need, but I'm not going to worry. Everything will work out. I'm just going to jump in there and get going."

Both of these approaches are wrong!

Before starting anything, we have to count the cost: "With the resources I have, can I accomplish this goal?" Without all the resources today, don't just jump off the deep end blindly assuming everything will just "work out." That's foolishness and self-centeredness. Because of timing, finances or other factors, you may have to wait a while to fully accomplish your plan or achieve your dream.

On the other hand, just because you don't have everything you need at the outset does not mean you cannot begin. Don't wait around until you have every resource you need or you will never start. Once you have identified the resources you need but don't have, you can begin the process to acquire those resources. In the meantime, begin with what you *do* have and work the parts that you already have the resources for.

Essentially, organization includes the assessment phase where you identify what you need that you already have, what you need that you do *not* already have and how you are going to get what you do not have.

After the plan is in place and organizing around the plan has been completed, the next step is *staffing*.

In the organizing phase, we begin to identify and create the systems that will ensure multiplication. The systems are the tools the staff must use to fulfill the goals and reach the vision. Your leadership team, which is selected in the next phase, will help you develop your systems. But it actually begins in the organization phase.

4. Staff

Staffing is when we match people to the task and the vision. Here is where we select the people needed to head up each area and complete each task. But this is also where we select people who are motivated by the vision. A person who has the right skill but is not motivated by the vision is the wrong person. He or she is a mere hireling motivated only by the money—which means you could lose that person if someone makes him or her a better offer.

Great teams are not built around the paycheck. Great teams are built around the vision. You can have workers who are there for the check, but your leaders have to be attached to the vision.

The best way to approach this step is to divide the project into different departments or areas of responsibility and then look for the right people to head those areas. I cannot stress this highly enough: Never, never, *never* select your team until you have identified the areas where each one will be working. Why? Because success depends on matching the right person to the right responsibility and that is not possible until you know what the responsibilities are.

Many leaders are reluctant to approach people to take on responsibilities out of a fear of imposing on their time. Don't worry about it. Believe it or not, most people really do want to serve. Most people want to be part of something significant and know that they are bringing value to other people's lives. Everybody wants to feel needed and valued, to know that they have something of worth to contribute. As a matter of fact, deep down, most people want to be challenged; they want to be given the opportunity to stretch and broaden themselves. This desire goes back to the whole issue of self-worth. As I said in the previous chapter, most people are willing to do anything or sacrifice anything for a sense of self-worth.

When undertaking the staffing phase, look for people with interests, skills and passion in each area. This should be a "no-brainer." What will happen if you put a person in charge of an area who has no interest in that area? Or who lacks the necessary skills? Or who has no passion for what you have asked him or her to do? One word: *failure*. And on top of failure, you run the risk of blowing out the people you recruited because no one likes to fail. No one likes to be placed in an area that is beyond their expertise or interests. Once they have failed because they were an inappropriate choice, it may be very difficult to get them involved the next time, even if it is for something for which they are better suited.

Any area, no matter what it is, will succeed *only* when led by a *passionate*, *committed* and *knowledgeable* leader. Passion without knowledge will fail. What good is a pep rally for a team that does-n't know how to play the game? What good are motivational sem-inars if there is no systematic training program in place? Passion is great, even necessary, but no amount of passion alone will com-pensate for the lack of basic task knowledge.

On the other hand, knowledge without passion or commitment will fail. People rarely respond to "facts." We humans are relational beings; we respond not just mind to mind, but heart to heart and spirit to spirit. Who are the teachers we remember the most fondly? The teachers who demanded something of us; the teachers who believed in us and taught us to believe in ourselves; the teachers who were passionate about teaching and about the subject and—most importantly—about their students! Who remembers the teachers whose classes were nothing but dull recitation of facts with no life or spirit? Any student can tell the difference.

Success depends on matching the right person to the right responsibility.

Makes sure that all the leaders you choose are passionate, knowledgeable and committed. Once they are in place, it is best to let them choose the people who will work with them. This is important for two reasons. First, they will have more control over finding people who will be a good "fit" for them, and second, because they are passionate about the area they are directing, they will very likely know better than you other people who share their passions and would make good team members.

5. Manage

Once the plan is in place and organized and staffing has been completed, the project enters the *management* phase. Very simply, this is where you define and establish your management plan. This answers the question, "How do we relate to leadership?" Management is your system of daily operating.

As leaders we need to clearly define for our people how we are going to manage them. This phase covers everything from the hiring process to the firing process. This is the "brass tacks" of the business world. Every person needs to know exactly what we expect of him (or her), who to go to when he has questions, where to go for help with resources, where to find the information he needs, what kind of training we will provide, etc. Everybody on the team or in the entire organization needs to know where the buck stops and with whom. All of this calls for clear communication in both directions and at every level.

Management is your system of daily operating.

Inadequate attention to the management phase greatly increases the risk of miscommunication and breakdown in the team process as well as the danger of team members "falling through the cracks" with problems that go unresolved.

A report came out several years ago that revealed that over one 18-month period, 1.5 million talented people dropped out of the church world in America. Surveys showed that they left for any one of several reasons. Leading the list was the fact that *they did not feel needed*. They were not given an opportunity to serve, so they left. This goes back to the fear many leaders have of imposing on someone to ask him or her to do something. True, some insecure leaders don't ask talented people to help because they don't want to feel threatened. By and large, however, we fail to ask people to serve because we don't think they will be willing. Most of the time they are, especially if they are asked to do something that is compatible with their passion, knowledge and gifts.

One common complaint of leaders and workers alike is that they were not adequately trained for the positions and responsibilities they were given. If people are not trained properly, they are not managed properly, and if they are not trained or managed properly, they do not feel safe. People believe that their job is only as important as the training they receive. If we do not train them, we are saying, "Your job is not important," and that's how they will treat it. Training is an indispensable part of the management process. Make sure everyone is properly trained, feels safe and knows where to go to for help.

Managers are not simply people who make people work; managers are the people who will model the principles and philosophies on the broadest level of the multiplication process. I once heard someone say that the billion-dollar business known as McDonald's is in the hands of that 18-year-old who waits on the customer.

That cashier is a long way from the corporate office. He or she will never sit in a boardroom and hear the dreams of the corporate leaders. No! It will be a manager who is entrusted with duplicating the entire process to the person who will interact with the customer. How people are managed puts the final period on the last sentence of the corporate dream!

6. Delegate

Delegation is where you make the assignments to those who have been instructed about the management plan. This is a crucial point. Until we have taught the people what the management process is, we are not ready to delegate. Disaster awaits the leader who delegates assignments to people who don't know where to go for help or who don't know the scope of their freedom, responsibility or liability. Only when training is complete and the management process is in place and functioning should delegation begin.

There are two things delegation is *not*. First of all, delegation is not asking people to do the jobs we don't want to do. Unfortunately, that's the concept many of us have about delegation. Getting someone else to do the "dirty" jobs or the "thankless" jobs or any of the other tasks we find unpleasant or consider "beneath" us may seem like an easy way out, but in the end it only breeds unrest, frustration and resentment.

Second, delegation is not simply telling people what we want them to do. As persons of dignity and worth, they have the right to know why. It is said that Socrates taught leadership by nurturing. He said, "Great leaders make leadership and delegation *learning experiences*."

Delegation, when used properly, is the place where new leaders are developed.

Do you remember all those times when Mom said, "Just do it because I said so?" Do you remember how you felt? If you're like me, you may have done the task, whatever it was, but you didn't like it and did just enough to get by. If we take the same approach as leaders, we'll get the same result from those we are trying to lead: minimum effort and mediocre results from a resentful spirit. Whenever people are given a job, it is vital that they understand *why* that job is important. The importance of their job gives them a feeling of importance to the organization and its overall goals.

Delegation, when used properly, is the place where new leaders are developed. It is the only testing ground we have to let new people spread their wings. Delegation is the test of the leaders as well as the worker.

Delegation is the time to let people know their freedom and their responsibility. If they are to perform well and successfully with confidence, they need to know exactly what they are free to do and not to do. Are they free to make independent decisions within the scope of their particular role or are they only to gather information and bring it back for someone else to make the decision? Are they free to expend their budget money as they see fit or do they have to prepare and submit a purchase request before making any expenditures?

They also need to know the scope of their responsibilities. Who are they accountable to? Who is accountable to them? What tasks are they directly responsible for performing and what tasks can they in turn delegate to others?

Delegation should always be *clear*. Otherwise a person may not do as much as we wanted them to or, at the other extreme, they may overstep their authority and do something we never intended for them to do. Again, this is another area where clear communication is vital. Clear delegation helps eliminate confusion, duplication of effort and breakdown of the process.

Delegation is a powerful thing. If we train people well and give them the tools they need to do the job, delegation becomes a place of empowerment, a place of passing along trust, where people have the opportunity to take the next step or rise to the next level.

> *Nothing is a success until it has been measured!*

7. Measure

Now we come to the two most neglected steps of the entire process: *measurement* and *reporting*. For some reason, it is hard for many leaders to understand the importance of these two elements. The truth is, if measurement and reporting are not done, it doesn't matter if all the preceding steps were done right; the project will eventually fail. Nothing is a success until it has been measured! There must be some verifiable standard of measurement to determine the degree of success or failure and to be able to make changes and adjustments to improve future performance. What are the future prospects for an athletic team that never analyzes its performance in the last game? No improvement and they will continue to make the same mistakes in the future.

Everyone involved with the project should understand how his or her progress and effectiveness will be measured. In so doing, the goal becomes tangible and understandable. It is very important to establish a fair and reasonable method of measuring every task. The standard of measurement and evaluation should be explained *up front*, not during or after the project, so that everyone knows at the outset what to expect. This knowledge will help people approach their task in a more responsible manner.

Another important principle about measurement is to *measure regularly*. Establish particular times or points in the project where measurement and evaluation take place to see how things are going. This helps keep everything on track. It also helps identify trouble spots while they are still small enough to correct easily.

Another benefit of regular measurement is in protecting the dignity and self-worth of the people doing the work. It's far better to find individuals who are a little bit behind and encourage them because they are so close than to wait until they have gotten so far behind that they have to be replaced. Such a development can damage their self-worth and self-confidence and potentially blow them out of any further usefulness. There's a saying in management circles: "It's a cinch by the inch but hard by the yard." Measure regularly. Don't allow people to get into a position to fail. The goal is not just for the project to succeed but for everyone involved to succeed. This preserves the balance between developing people and accomplishing goals.

8. Reporting

The *reporting* stage is where you define how and when reporting will be done and to whom. Non-management people have a hard time understanding the importance of reporting after each project is completed. Why report? What's the big deal?

Reporting is essential because as leaders we are trying to bring congruence to everything we do and everything the organization does. This effort depends *entirely* on accurate reporting. Without reports we cannot know where the problems are that need to be fixed. Without reporting we have no way of measuring and rewarding success. More importantly, we have no way of knowing for sure if congruence has been achieved. Is everything running smoothly just as it should or has something gotten off track somewhere? Are all departments working together or are some laboring at cross-purposes with each other? What needs to be fixed? What can we improve? Are there any "holes" in the process that need to be plugged? How can we do this more effectively the next time? Without accurate reports from *every* department, these questions are impossible to answer...and the same mistakes will be repeated!

Most leaders today do not believe reporting is essential. The fact is, leaders who do not require reports are failing and do not even know it. Without reporting there can be no effective measuring and without effective measuring there can be no true success. Their team will fall apart under their leadership because where there is no reporting, people feel no sense of accountability or that the buck stops anywhere. Instead, they feel that they are self-managed.

Leaders who do not require reports are failing and do not even know it.

People who fail to report when required are almost always failing to produce. Leaders who have people responsible for reporting to them cannot afford to assume otherwise. No leader should have to track down a person to get a report. If so, that person needs to be replaced. Reporting is *that* important!

These are the Eight Critical Factors of Success. Even if nothing else in your organization is done perfectly, master these eight steps and your success is virtually guaranteed. Productivity will increase, morale will rise, self-confidence among the entire team will grow, people will be developed, goals will be reached—and you will become a successful, effective leader.

Chapter Four

WHERE DO YOU WANT TO GO?

<figure>⟨ᴢ∞ᴢ⟩</figure>

E very leader is driven by something. Deep in the heart of
every leader is a catalyst, a motivating factor that drives
everything he or she does. At its core, a leader's motivation
derives, as we saw in Chapter Two, from his or her sense of identity and self-worth. A flawed sense of identity and self-worth
drives a leader to seek those things in externals such as performance or approval from others. In the minds of such leaders, people become commodities, disposable tools for the leaders to use
in building their own self-esteem and accomplishing their own
personal dreams and goals.

Leaders with a healthy self-worth, on the other hand, are free
to serve and build up others because their own self-valuation
derives from a source not connected to performance or the need
for approval. From this perspective, they view other people not as
commodities but as valuable assets, persons of dignity and worth
with dreams and goals of their own as well as gifts, talents, abilities, knowledge and insight that are crucial to the success of the

organization. The leader who has strong self-worth is able to allow others to get honor from their work. They share the glory just as they share the responsibility.

Unfortunately, our modern society is burdened with far too many leaders of the first type and blessed with far too few of the second. This imbalance is found in every area and at every level of leadership, whether the ministry, the corporate and business sector or the political realm. It is this vacuum of people who have a healthy sense of self-worth that enable insecure people to force their way into leadership roles, seeking to meet their own needs at the expense of others and thereby crippling the workforce in America.

Insecure leaders seem to fall into two general categories: *poll-driven* leaders and *policy-driven* leaders. Poll-driven leaders decide where they stand based on the latest public opinion polls or surveys. They also could be called "windmill leaders" because their position depends on which way the wind is blowing. How can such leaders possibly chart a course for others to follow—much less inspire them to follow—when they are constantly changing direction themselves? Such a *leader* is not a leader at all. He (or she) is actually following the people and making it appear that he is leading.

In recent years this kind of leadership has been particularly evident in the political arena with office-holders who seem to have no strong convictions of their own but depend on the results of polls to help them decide which side of the fence to come down on. Such "government by poll" seems to be common among political leaders whose primary concern is not leadership or doing the right thing but getting re-elected.

For policy-driven leaders the *program* is the main thing; for some, in fact, it is the *only* thing. Everything and everyone in the organization exists to serve the program. Nothing matters except productivity; everything centers on making deadlines and reaching quotas. Not only are personal needs, vision and dreams secondary, but they are irrelevant.

Virtually all of us have at one time or another either seen or worked for this kind of leader: insecure and paranoid from an "I am disposable" mentality that drives them to focus on performance only and to demand the same from everybody else.

At the other end of the spectrum is the *people-driven* leader: secure, confident, self-assured and committed equally to the corporate vision, goals of the organization and the personal vision and dreams of the people. For this kind of leader success is not a matter of either-or but both-and. He or she understands that a balance between corporate goals and personal development is not only possible but essential before he or she can legitimately claim success.

A people-driven leader also acknowledges that achieving such a balance requires a set of carefully and clearly defined goals as well as a systematic plan for reaching those goals and for regular monitoring of progress along the way. We looked at all these elements in the previous chapter.

In order for this process to work, the leader must begin by asking the questions, "Where do I want to go?" and "How are we going to get there?" The answers to these questions will determine both the direction and the character of the team that leader puts together.

Set Your Destination

With any organization or project, it is rare for every goal to be crystal clear at the start. This is not necessarily a bad thing. Every human undertaking evolves as it develops. Some goals will become clear only after the plan is in process. Other goals may require periodic re-clarification or even change. Not only is this perfectly acceptable, but it also is to be expected. However, the less clear the vision, the less probability of proper planning, organizing and staffing. We can know what skills are needed only to the degree that we know our destination. It is acceptable to adjust our plan as we go, but it is *not* acceptable to *go* until we have our destination clearly in mind.

We cannot plan, organize or staff until we know where we are going. If we want to travel the surface of the moon, we will need a rocket to get there, a lunar vehicle for travel once we arrive, space suits, enough oxygen to last the entire trip, a lot of supplies and some very talented people in specific areas. On the other hand, if all we want to do is travel across town, the only thing we need is a car with a quarter tank of gas. Until we know where we want to go, we do not know who or what it will take to get there. Planning, organization and staffing are impossible until we know where we are going.

Even the best and most highly trained staff of professionals will be useless to us if they are improperly equipped to assist us in reaching our particular destination. Not only will they be of no help, they also will be a hindrance. A group of automobile specialists could build the highest ramp in the world and the fastest car ever designed; they could be the best in their field, but if we are attempting a lunar launch, we have the wrong team. This particular group of highly trained professionals would cost us our lives. Sure, they are good at what they do, but they are good at the wrong things—at least for our needs.

Many times the lack of a clear-cut goal is the result of fear. Some leaders fail to clarify their goals out of fear of failure, fear of criticism or fear of making a mistake. Any person who will not commit to a specific destination is not walking in a leadership role. He (or she) is a follower, no matter what his title may be. Instead of leading in a specific direction, he waits to see where the staff is going and then moves to the head of the parade. This is a lot like shooting an arrow into a tree and then drawing a bull's-eye around it. The team's destination is wherever they happen to be pointed at the moment.

Such a person cannot build a team or develop leaders. He may amass a group of people, but they will not be a team. Undirected, they will head off on their own path leaving him perplexed and wondering which way they went.

For example, it is not uncommon for a church to have many sects or cliques within its congregation. Often times each group will have opposing beliefs and a different vision. This lack of congruency gives rise to division and strife that, if allowed to continue unchecked, often brings about a church split if not the dissolving of the entire congregation. The same is true in business or any other organization with weak leadership.

The lack of a clear-cut goal is often the result of fear.

Having a clearly defined destination may lessen the number of people who will walk with us, but it will increase the level of commitment and team spirit. Fewer qualified people will be far more effective by being part of a synergistic team than will a larger group of people who have the wrong skills. People want leadership. They want to know where the team is going. Only then can they step forward and identify how their passion can be fulfilled on the team. People without a clear-cut goal are always half-hearted and reluctant. They lack passion, drive and a sense of purpose. If they do not know where they are going, it is only a matter of time before they start asking, "Why am I here?" In time this leads to feelings of pointlessness and low productivity. People with purpose produce!

The Paradox of Successful Staffing

It is at this point that we confront a reality that is the paradox of successful staffing: Every person must fulfill his or her individual passion, yet every person also must be fully committed to the goals of the team and the organization. This produces a synergy that exceeds anything any of us could accomplish on our own. In a synergistic environment, two or more distinctive factors come together and, while maintaining their individual function and identity, become something new that they could never become alone. Synergy, then, results in a product that is greater than the sum of its individual parts. Absence of synergy, on the other hand, creates a centrifugal force that scatters instead of gathers. It pulls any organization in opposing directions, giving rise to weakness, division and eventual destruction.

Successful leadership teams must have certain factors. Everyone must see the "big picture." Everyone must understand the role they play in the accomplishment of the overall vision. Every team member must be committed to reaching the common goal, while at the same time fulfilling their own personal passions.

Everyone must fulfill his or her passion yet be fully committed to the goals of the team.

Whenever we bring staff into a leadership position, it is essential that their passion and goals be consistent with ours. Likewise, their commitment to fulfilling our passion must not prevent them from fulfilling theirs. They are, after all, becoming a part of a team. A group of men wearing the same uniform do not make a football team. They will not be a team until they are all running toward the same goal. If they want to be a successful, winning team, they must pursue the common goal while each one individually does what he does best. They all have to know all the plays, but they do not all play the same position. You can't have a team with all quarterbacks. Each team member has a specific position he is best at. He may be able to play several positions well, but he usually stands out on one specific area—and that is where he is best utilized. Working together this way, a team creates synergy and truly becomes a team. Each team member plays a different position that he loves, but everyone has the same purpose.

As leaders we need to understand that there is a fine line between control and leading. We never want to dominate. We never want to misuse people. Yet, we must fulfill our passion. How we build our team will force us to be either a controller or a leader. Knowing where we are going and selecting people who have a passion for the area in which they are needed are the keys to never becoming a controller. If we choose the wrong team players, or if we put the wrong people in the wrong positions, we will always be forcing people instead of leading people.

There will always be people who want to be a part of our team. We must be wise enough to make good personnel decisions. We must have a process whereby we identify and prove a person's skill, passion and character. This is for our good as well as theirs. Everyone does not need to be on our team. Regardless of their talent and skill, they may be the wrong person for the job. It is always better to have a less talented, passionate person in the right spot than to have a very talented, passionless person in the wrong spot. An unfulfilled person always becomes trouble. Someone once said, "One person with a passion is greater than ninety-nine with only interest."

Too often people are brought into a position because of their personal loyalty to the leader. This is an environment that breeds co-dependency and deceit. A wise leader wants people who have a high commitment to their own passion. I do not want a leader on my team who would abandon his or her passion just to be on my staff. Likewise, the leader who has foresight wants each team member to be more committed to the goal than to the leader. A person who is committed to the cause will be faithful whether the leader is present or absent. A secure leader realizes the importance of personal commitment but also recognizes where such commitment ranks on the priority scale. For leaders who are committed to the big picture, personal commitment to them on the part of team members is less important than the members' commitment to the goal.

Often we allow our fears, insecurities and ambitions to control us. Out of greed, we want everyone on our team. We do not want to let the good ones go, so we "trouble our own house." We undermine our own dream by putting good people in the wrong slots. Thinking we can change them, we end up trying to manipulate their passions. We think we can make them faithful to our dreams. Time always reveals that a person who is willing to be untrue to his or her own dreams can never be trusted to share the dreams of another.

Regardless of their skill and talent, people's passion must be consistent with ours if they are to make good team members. They must want the same end result that we want. They are not wrong if they do not want to fulfill our passion; they are just not right for us. Not every person is going to be the quarterback. Not every person is going to carry the ball, but everyone on the team has to love football and have the desire to win.

It is absolutely essential that people understand how they can fulfill their passions by becoming a part of our team. None of us would coerce a fast basketball player into carrying the football for us. Every time we would think he was about to score, he would try to dribble the ball. Our team members need to play the game and position they desire, not the ones we desire for them.

Too many times talented people have been asked to give up their dream for that of the leader. This is completely wrong. As leaders we should never ask or expect people to give up their own dreams. Our dream will not motivate them. Its accomplishment will not fulfill them. Instead, they will become the ones who require constant encouragement and motivation. They will be the ones who want to quit every time it gets hard. They will be the ones who are never really with us.

Our Vision Must Facilitate the Fulfillment of Theirs

One common complaint I hear from leaders and managers around the world is, "I cannot get the people to be diligent and committed. I cannot find people who have a passion for anything." Too often the problem turns out to be not a lack of passion but the fact that people are being manipulated to do something they really do not want to do. The only reason they do it is because the leader wants it. Herein lies the difference between a manipulator and a motivator. A manipulator encourages others to do what he or she desires. A motivator encourages others to do what they desire.

Too often a leader makes everyone else feel that they must share his or her specific passion. We insist that they must love what we love. Such an environment produces guilt, condemnation and frustration: "If I do not want what the leader wants, there must be something wrong with me." Not only do they fail to have a passion for our dreams, they also soon lose passion for their own dreams. By exalting our dreams above the dreams of others, we become "dream stealers."

The problem is usually not lack of passion, but manipulation.

Once we have stolen their dreams, they will become frustrated, passionless, purposeless, unmotivated people doomed for failure. Their failure will contribute to our failure, and in the end our selfish ambitions will prevent all of us from living our dreams.

As leaders with integrity, we must first know where we are going. We must have a plan to get there. We must organize around that plan and then staff to meet those organizational needs. Those staff members, whether volunteer or paid, must have a vision that will complement ours. At the same time, our vision must facilitate the fulfillment of theirs.

A good front door is the only cure for a bad back door. Staffing—hiring the right people—is the cure. Hiring people who do not have the skill, the passion or a complementary vision always leads to an undesirable outcome. Leaders who hire fast always live to regret it. Hire slow and fire fast. That is the best thing for both the organization and the people!

Just as a conscientious parent encourages a child to fulfill his or her own passions, a benevolent leader will seek to know and understand the passions of those he (or she) leads. He will seek to place those people in areas where their personal passions are fulfilled. Then it becomes a win-win situation. The staff members win because they get to fulfill their dreams. The leader and the organization win because their goal is fulfilled. All of this is the product of knowing where we are going and finding those who can walk with us while at the same time fulfilling their dreams.

Some studies indicate that people will work for less pay if they are fulfilled in other areas. People who are doing what they enjoy will sacrifice with the organization when necessary. Those who are living their dream will be the last ones to leave the ship even when it appears to be sinking. Commitment is the fruit of a fulfilled person, not the magic motivation of an inspired leader.

Like-Minded Leaders

Having leaders who are of one mind and purpose is absolutely essential. Being like-minded does not mean that we agree on everything. It does not mean that we have the same behavior patterns. It means that we are in agreement in the essential areas. I highly value the diversity of my staff. I want to be surrounded by people who think differently than I. If we all see everything the same way, we have too many weaknesses and blind spots. Our diversity of perception and opinion is a great strength. It virtually guarantees that any discussion will produce ideas or angles I would never have thought of. A strong leader is never threatened by differences of opinion. Instead he or she welcomes the diversity.

A leadership team does not function like a denomination or political party. We do not exist to maintain or reinforce our opinions. It is not about providing strength for weak leaders who need the false security of agreement. Mature leaders will surround themselves with those who know how to challenge and disagree in a mature way. "Yes men" are the destruction of too many organizations. The moral, ethical and financial failure of too many leaders is the fruit of the "yes men" team. A healthy leadership team will nurture and challenge one another. Their commitment to the cause prevents them from being "yes men." They are not willing to let the leader ruin the dream. They are protecting the organization's dream because it is also their own.

I remember once being called upon for consultation work with a particular ministry leader. He had a key spot in his ministry that he could not keep filled. Every time he found a person who seemed to be right for the job, he soon discovered weaknesses that made the person unacceptable for the position. This man was a typical insecure leader who did not like to be challenged. He was accustomed to surrounding himself with those who always agreed with him.

Being like-minded does not mean that we agree on everything.

My advice to him was simple: "When you find someone who has the needed skills, he will probably be someone you will not like on a personal level. The skills needed to fill this slot will not be found in a typical 'yes man.' You are making the decisions for this person. Therefore, he is not able to do his job. The reason he agrees with all of your decisions is because he is just like you. You both see everything the same way. That means you both have the same weaknesses and therefore the same blind spots. You both forget the same things. You both make the same mistakes. Stop hiring people because they are like you. Stop hiring people to be your buddy. Hire someone who has the skills to do the job—a job that you or someone like you does not have the skill to do."

Once we get past the fact that we want diversity and once we find a person who has the necessary qualifications, the next step is to make sure that we are like-minded in the crucial areas. More than anything else, we want to know that this person will be a servant-leader who will always seek what is best for the people. Paul had this same concern when he wrote to the Philippian church:

But I trust in the Lord Jesus to send Timothy to you shortly, that I also may be encouraged when I know your state. For I have no one like-minded, who will sincerely care for your state. For all seek their own, not the things which are of Christ Jesus (Philippians 2:19-21).

In every area of life, ministry and business, leaders must be willing to live for a cause, seek the care of those they serve and preserve their own sense of dignity and worth. Otherwise we are not leaders at all; we are simply self-centered controllers. Remember, this is not a win-lose proposition but an opportunity for everybody to win. In every situation every person should walk away having benefited him or herself and others. We must have leaders whom we know will serve the people and the cause.

One of the greatest weaknesses of most organizations is in the development and promotion of leaders. Every successful organization must have some system of developing leaders that is balanced with didactic training, modeling, supervised application and ongoing development. Each person on a team or a staff must be highly qualified in his or her particular skills, yet also be fully committed to serving.

Everyone looks good on paper. Too many times, however, the application and the references are a far cry from reality. As leaders in the new millennium we must accept an undeniable reality: If we desire a leadership team that is highly skilled, highly trained, highly motivated *and* committed to serving people, *we must develop them*. Unfortunately, few schools, colleges, seminaries or churches today actually train anyone to serve anymore.

Like-minded leaders are developed through a consistent, systematic, developmental program. Even those who come with all the proper credentials and saying all the right things usually require development. With patience and careful attention to the developmental process we can surround ourselves with a diverse group of people who are committed to the same cause and are governed by the same values, yet who maintain their individual identity and passion.

Pursuing Effectiveness

When a diverse team of highly trained, highly motivated and highly passionate people set out together for a common goal, it is vital that everyone, and particularly the team leader, be committed to *effectiveness*. This is a deliberate decision that we all must make as we pursue our calling and dreams. Too often we assume that we have made that decision.

Only very rarely have I ever had a leader tell me that he or she had made a conscious, deliberate, definite commitment to effectiveness. Most often the answer is, "Of course I want to be effective." What leader doesn't? That's not the point. The question is not, "Do you want to be effective?" but "Have you made a *commitment* to effectiveness?" People are committed to growth. They are committed to prayer. They are committed to many very noble and essential things. But rarely does a person make a deliberate, conscious, quantified commitment to effectiveness. It's just not something most people think about.

It's something leaders *must* think about. Thinking leads to commitment, commitment leads to action and action leads to results. Studies show that when people *set their intention* to learn something, they actually increase their capacity to learn by 1100 percent! Likewise, any time we set our intention in *any* area, our success rate increases significantly and our learning curve decreases.

Effectiveness and success are easily confused. Although they go hand in hand, they are not the same. One is cause and the other is effect. A commitment to effectiveness always ends in success. However, the desire to succeed apart from a commitment to effectiveness has left many leaders in despair and disappointment. Failure to commit to a defined standard of effectiveness is a major factor in genuine efforts not reaching fruition. It often lies at the heart of the failure of otherwise good programs. Starting a program without a deliberate commitment to effectiveness is like trying to build a house without referring to the blueprints. By itself, our desire to succeed is not enough. We must consciously commit ourselves to effectiveness.

According to George Barna, only 20 percent of evangelical churches in America consider themselves successful. Out of 320,000 evangelical churches, only 64,000 are succeeding, according to their own evaluations. In other words, they are not able to accomplish the goals they set out to accomplish.

Effectiveness is something leaders must think about.

In Chapter One I discussed the fact that a faulty definition of success will prevent us from ever being truly effective. Sometimes our mental image of success is only measured in quantity with little regard for quality. In many cases, our definition of success actually leads us *away* from true effectiveness.

Commitment to quality means more than just the quality of the program. It is a commitment to the quality that the program brings to the lives of people, whether congregation, customers or clients. While seeking to fulfill the goals of our organization, we also must be fully committed to contributing to the quality of life of the people to whom we minister or who use our products or services. Is this why we do what we do? Do we qualify every program and every project and every service by the quality it brings to the lives of the recipients or consumers, as well as for the benefit it brings to our organization?

Assessing Our Opportunities

One immediate benefit of a commitment to effectiveness is that it makes a leader more sensitive and alert to opportunities that come along that will help the team on its journey toward the goal. As a matter of fact, all the elements we have been talking about— a clear destination, clearly defined goals, like-minded leadership and diversity of passion, dreams and talents among team members—enhance the entire group's ability to capitalize on opportunities that less congruent groups are likely to miss.

Opportunities surround us in abundance. Unfortunately opportunities and obstacles often look so much alike that only our attitude will allow us to see the difference. Regular assessment of our situation can lead us to current opportunities that will take us to the next level of growth and effectiveness. This is one of the reasons periodic measurement, one of the Eight Critical Factors of Success, is so critical. If we want to capitalize on opportunities, we have to position ourselves to be able to do so. This requires continual monitoring so we will know where we are and what our condition is at any given moment.

Opportunities and obstacles often look so much alike that only our attitude will allow us to see the difference.

I am a vision-oriented person. Thirty years ago I saw a picture in my heart, and I have pursued it with passionate diligence. Regardless of how clearly I saw the end from the beginning, it didn't take me very long to realize that knowing the destination and recognizing the path are two entirely different things. I think this is the major challenge for every leader. Knowing the target is simple; finding the way to get there is a continually evolving process.

Quantum physics poses a dilemma that is mirrored in life. Physicists have discovered that taking measurements at the quantum level is extremely difficult because the very process of measuring changes the conditions they are trying to measure. In the same way, our ability to measure and understand is changed based on where we are when we measure. Our position alters our perception. The Empire State Building looks very different from the street below than it does from across the Hudson River. With every advancement we make toward our goal, our perception or understanding of how we will meet that goal changes. Every time we move forward, the path looks a little different. From each new vantage point our perception changes. Therefore, we as leaders are faced with the need to constantly re-evaluate and make adjustments.

In this regard, two of the greatest keys to success are flexibility and adaptability. Flexible leaders are open to new thoughts and ideas. They do not become rigid in their point of view. It is not as important to them to *be* right as it is to discover what *is* right. They are able to hold fast to the goal while at the same time adjusting to new insights. With every fresh new perspective, flexible leaders are able to adapt their plan to their new insight.

Adjusting Course

When learning underwater diving, I also had to learn how to chart a course with the compass. I would get a reading, then go underwater and try to find my destination. It was incredibly challenging! Occasionally I would realize that I had stopped paying attention to my compass. Sometimes I had no idea how far off course I had gotten. There were several occasions where this forced me in desperation to return to the surface to take another compass reading before making another attempt to reach my destination. From this new location my whole perception would change. Although I was headed to the same destination, the compass reading would be different. Why? Simple! I was viewing the destination from a new vantage point.

As leaders, we must regularly adjust our course from our new vantage point. Assessing our situation by surveys, questions, comments and even complaints is the only way we will be able to take a regular, fresh look at our current location and adjust the course to ensure we are still on track.

It is vitally important that we assess our effectiveness regularly. At Impact we regularly assess our church, ministry and every other aspect of what we do. I am often surprised by new developments. For example, not long ago we moved into a new facility. This change brought about a shift in the types of people who walked through our doors. For years we had a need for a strong youth group because the median age of our church members and visitors fell into a group that had teenage children.

A recent survey revealed that the second largest age group visiting our church was families with children from infant to 12 years of age. From the pulpit, this shift was not apparent; nor was it apparent based on the group of people I talked to. But the statistics don't lie. We have a new emerging need in our church.

The largest group walking through our doors today are singles or what we call the "college and career" age. Interestingly enough, most of these single adults are divorced. In order to effectively keep and disciple these groups, we had to adjust our emphasis. Our overall goal was the same: reach people with the message and ministry of the love of God in Jesus Christ. It was the *type* of people and the demographics that were changing, and we had to change our approach accordingly or lose our effectiveness.

We leaders must regularly adjust our course from our new vantage points.

What changes are going on in and around your organization? What adjustments do you need to make to take those changes into account and continue to be effective? How will you know? Here are some suggestions.

Ask questions. Always ask questions. Do it in conversations. Do it in surveys. Do it through visitor/customer information. Have a suggestion box not only for workers but also for customers or clients. Ask for honest assessments of your personal effectiveness as a leader as well as the overall effectiveness of your team or organization in meeting goals, delivering what is promised and responding to problems and complaints.

Asking questions is a masterful art. In fact, when you ask questions and show a genuine interest in others, they will think that you are the most interesting person they have ever met. As you talk to people, whether face to face or through correspondence of some kind, listen attentively to their answers and you will discover vast amounts of information that you can use to become more effective in the future.

Adjust your plans. What worked yesterday may not be effective today. Outreach or marketing programs that worked in the

1960's, 70's, 80's or 90's are not necessarily effective today. What worked in one city may not work in another. Every time you make an assessment, it will force you to refine your plan. Don't put efforts in place just because it was effective *once*. Your job as a leader is to discover what is effective *now*.

How have the demographics for your organization changed? Have you relocated? Has your client base or the makeup of your congregation changed? Have new subdivisions or apartments been built in your area? Has your company expanded? Downsized? All of these kinds of changes call for a reassessment and probable readjustment of your plan and your goals.

Put your efforts in the place of greatest opportunity. Regardless of how good you and your team are in a particular area, to be successful with the least amount of effort means you must identify the areas of immediate opportunity and adjust to seize the moment.

One of my favorite leadership scriptures is 1 Chronicles 12:32, which refers to some of the people who accompanied King David. It describes the men of Issachar as those who *"had understanding of the times, to know what Israel ought to do."* One of the reasons David was such an effective and successful king is that he surrounded himself with wise and effective leaders. I believe this is one of the greatest needs in both the church and corporate worlds today: people who understand the times and are able to adapt to seize new opportunities.

Do not try function under the old adage, "The squeaky wheel gets the grease." Don't put your efforts where there is the greatest need. Put your efforts where there is the greatest *opportunity*. Ecclesiastes 3:1 says, *"To everything there is a season, a time for every purpose under heaven."* Understand your season and plant accordingly!

Gather visitor/customer/client information. Always make sure you know who is walking through your doors or using your products or services and *why*. What do they like? What do they dislike? How could you improve? What do they need or want that you could supply but are not currently doing so?

Plan your outreach/marketing. If your customer information tells you where people are hearing about your church, business or organization, you now know where your natural market exists. Your most effective marketing/outreach strategy would be to focus on the group that is already the most responsive.

Take a fresh look at your facilities and customer service. Because of the way our mind works, we stop noticing what we see every day. For example, there may be some eyesore that every visitor encounters when they come onto your property or enter your building. Yet, you walk past it every week and no longer notice it. As a means of survival, the mind stops noticing things that once caused irritation.

Get a "secret shopper" to visit your church or establishment to observe your environment and procedures and interact with your staff. This is a technique employed by many large restaurant chains. They hire people to visit their restaurants and evaluate everything. These people notice what the regulars have come to accept. They provide a fresh set of eyes and a fresh perspective. A secret shopper can identify the unintentional signals you are sending to visitors or customers. Remember, what the regulars have come to accept will turn a newcomer away!

Learn to properly assess the situation and you will see an abundance of new opportunities. I always think of the story of the two shoe salesmen who flew to a distant island in search of new markets. When they arrived, the first salesman called the home office and said, "I'm coming back. There is no opportunity for us here. No one on this island wears shoes." The second called the home office and said, "You can't believe the opportunity here! Send me everything you've got in the warehouse! Nobody here has shoes."

What new opportunities are in front of you? Make a commitment to seize them today!

Chapter Five

RECRUITING A WINNING TEAM

Recruiting is the first active step toward team building. As leaders, we are team builders; that is our primary function. Continuing success depends on continually building teams and developing leaders. Any leader who is not focused on recruiting and team building is defaulting toward failure. This is because without recruiting, attrition will eventually win out over any temporary success.

Nothing in life is static. Life is always changing, yet many people still look for that elusive place called "there." Whether in their marriage, their business, their team or their church they think, "Once I get 'there' I'll be fine." "Just a little while longer and I'll be 'there', and then I'll have it made." The only problem with this idea is that once we get "there," we will only be "there" for a few days at most and then everything will change again. Our life circumstances are always changing. Whoever said, "The only constant in life is change" was absolutely right.

Because life is always changing, in order to have true success in every area of life we must adopt a dynamic, proactive lifestyle where day by day we feel our way through whatever it takes to be effective that day. We can't automatically rely on what worked yesterday. Values and morals stay the same. Principles stay the same. But the application of all those factors is adjusted daily to work in an ever-changing world!

For example, what it takes for my wife Brenda and me to have a good marriage today is quite different from what it was years ago. Back then, I expected Brenda to iron my clothes and cook all my meals. At that time it was a reasonable expectation because she was not employed outside the home. Since then, circumstances have changed. Today, like me, Brenda is very busy outside the home. Quite often now I iron my own clothes and fix my own breakfast because that is what the current dynamic of our lives calls for. Life is always changing, and we need to be ready to change with it.

The same thing is true of the teams we build. Attrition is simply the natural fallout or losses that occur in any team, business, church or other organization. If you have a business, you're going to continually lose customers for one reason or another. It's a fact of life. For that reason, if you don't want your business to die, you must continually gain new customers. In business, as in life, you can't afford to rest on your laurels. Your current customers will move, die, find a better offer, get offended or change their mind about what they want. Never stop growing. Never stop recruiting team members.

At Impact, we lose more stable families to job transfers than any other single reason. People we have loved and worked hard to build and develop and who have contributed much to the life and ministry of our church are suddenly gone. That's simple attrition and it's unavoidable. Sure, I could get mad. I could pout or whine about losing such good folks, but it will still happen. The solution is not to complain or to get upset but to continue recruiting, continue building and continue developing people.

Attrition will always occur, so recruiting and building must be a continuing process as well.

No matter what your organization, unless you are continually growing, you are continually shrinking. Anything that is alive grows, and when it stops growing it starts dying. Inflexibility leading to rigidity is one of the first visible signs of death in any living organism. If you are a leader who has experienced success, don't rest on that success. Don't assume that your last success bought you some time to "coast." Otherwise that success will become a frustrating, embittering failure when natural attrition causes you to lose some of the people you have built up and developed so carefully. No matter how large your success, it is only temporary if you are not recruiting.

Basics of Team Building

A team is a group of skilled people organized to work together, committed to the same goal, working the same plan, who are properly positioned to use their skill. This simple definition actually provides a good outline for leaders to use in team building.

First of all, team members must be *skilled*. This is accomplished through a careful hiring/screening/training process. No one should end up on a team who does not possess the skills needed for success on that team. Secondly, the team must be *organized*. Among other things, this means making sure that all team members understand their function and where their work fits in the overall process of team operation. Thirdly, each team member must be committed to the same *goal*, which means they have to go through systems training. Fourthly, team members must work the same *plan*. This means they have to experience a management process that they understand. And finally, they must be *properly positioned*. In other words, the work they do on the team must match their skills and passion.

When it comes to effective team building, leaders function more as coaches than anything else. Great coaches are always team builders. They may not even necessarily have been the best *players* in their day. Their greatness lies not so much in their personal ability to play the game but in their ability to recruit and build winning teams.

Here in Alabama, whenever we think of great coaches, the name of Paul "Bear" Bryant comes immediately to mind. "Bear" Bryant, of course, was one of the "winningest" football coaches in NCAA history and an outstanding leader and team builder. A former player of Bryant's described to me the secrets of his success. He said that Coach Bryant was so successful because he recruited the best players, was a great motivator and surrounded himself with talented leaders.

> *For effective team building, leaders function more as coaches than anything else.*

That's a great prescription for success in any area or endeavor of life! When you boil it down, those really are the only three elements necessary for success as a coach or leader: recruit the best people, surround yourself with talent and focus on motivation. If you want to build a team or a business like a coach, these are the elements you will have to bring into the process.

Establish the Same Goals for Everybody

Our ability to build teams rests solely in our ability to identify, recruit and train workers and leaders. What's the difference between training a leader and a worker? *Nothing.* There is no difference. As leaders we set the same goals for everybody. The Bible lists several specific qualities required for those who would be leaders in the church, such as deacons, elders, ministers, etc. As it turns out, those standards are no different than the standards given for good, common Christian living. There's nothing special about the goals for a leader compared to the goals for a worker. Leadership training is also training for life, so it is appropriate for everyone.

The journey to becoming an effective leader is the same journey for learning how to live a stable, effective, fruitful life. There is therefore little difference between the training of leaders and the training of workers. The difference comes in the fact that the people with leadership potential and desire start taking self-initiating steps. They begin using their influence and become very proactive.

Some of you might be saying about now, "Well, I'm just not a recruiter. I'm no good at recruiting; I don't enjoy recruiting; I'm not even confident I can evaluate people's potential well enough to become a good recruiter." Guess what? *You* don't necessarily have to *be* the recruiter. "Bear" Bryant probably personally recruited very few football players in his long career, unless it was some "mega-star" high school player on whom he wanted to use his personal influence. He *had* recruiters. All college and pro teams have recruiters. We call them scouts. They go out and look for talent to recruit.

> *There is no difference between training a leader and a worker.*

Being a leader or senior team leader doesn't necessarily mean you have to personally do all of these things as long as you are totally committed to making sure they *are* done by someone on your team. If you are not a recruiter, figure out who needs to be the scout for your business or ministry. I can't stress this enough: If you are not recruiting or making sure that it happens on your team or in your business, then your team or business is dying. That's simply the way it is.

Work the System!

Every successful team and organization of any kind has a system: a systematic approach to recruiting, training and appointing leaders and workers. A system only works, however, when it is used consistently. That's why it is called a system.

Working the system successfully means, among other things, avoiding actions that work at cross-purposes to the system, thereby breaking it. In this regard there are at least four "nevers" to observe when recruiting:

1. Never overlook anyone.

2. Never prejudge who will succeed.

3. Never make decisions based on feelings.

4. Never position a person based on potential.

All four of these are linked. Never overlook anyone because you cannot tell by appearance or personality alone who has "it" and who doesn't. Never prejudge people because you never know who will make it and who won't. For the same reason, never choose a leader based on your personal feelings for that person. Your job as a leader is to find the best person for each position. It has nothing to do with friendship. If you make selections based on prejudgments or feelings, I guarantee you will always choose the wrong people. The reason for this has to do with the fourth "never": Never position a person based on potential.

I've had people say to me, "Man, I want you to know that I am committed to this church. You can call on me anytime for anything, day or night, and I'll be ready. This is what I'm going to do. I'm going to make so much happen in this church." Well, we have a saying in the part of the world I come from: "When the check clears the bank, it's real."

People will come to you and say a lot of things and even show a lot of potential. The greatest frustration you will ever experience is when you pass positive judgments about people, make assumptions and, based on their potential, assume that they will deliver the goods, only to discover, when you give them the chance, that they don't.

One of the points I cannot stress enough to leaders is, *work the system*. The system is designed to ensure that only people who are trained and prepared enter leadership positions, but it won't work if it's not used.

Time after time I have had people sitting across the desk from me complaining that nobody's committed and that nobody wants to do anything. That's when I ask, "Did you take this person through the orientation before you ever put him [or her] to work?" "No." "Did you model what you wanted that person to do?" "No." When you get down to it, you find out that the person had potential. "He looked sharp, so I thought he could do it." In the end, what they did was defaulted away from working any part of the system. Nearly every time I have violated my own system for recruiting and developing potential leaders, it has blown up in my face. The system is there to save you, not punish you!

I cannot stress enough the importance of working the system.

The way you keep from judging, making assumptions and going on feelings, is simply to work the system. Have predictable steps through which people must journey toward the next step. Don't let people take shortcuts, especially in the beginning. Proverbs sets forth a principle that says if you treat someone too easy up front, he'll want to be treated like a son in the end. The people who work the system are the people who will produce the goods for you. The people who will not go through a system will not. If you give someone a break in the system, never let it be in the beginning.

One of the questions pastors all over the world ask me is, "Why have you never had a church split?" The number one reason? To get into leadership on a serious level at Impact, particularly a staff level of leadership, everyone has to go through a system. The people who are power brokers and users of people and egotistical will not work a system. They always want you to treat them special and give them a shortcut. It's not that I'm so insightful or that I've done so much that is right; this is just one thing I happen to have done right. And because of that, all the people who had another agenda always faded out; they eventually got frustrated before they ever got far into working the system. They revealed their motives when they couldn't take shortcuts. You can have a great team if you will simply work the system and refuse judgments and assumptions.

Recruit Up!

Another must is always *recruit up!* We all have a tendency to recruit down. By recruiting down, I mean that our tendency is to look for people less skilled or less talented than we are. If we find somebody who is already functioning at some higher level of professionalism, we sometimes feel a little intimidated at the idea of bringing somebody like that onto our team. It isn't always intimidation; sometimes it is ego. We're reluctant to bring somebody on who is more talented than we are because we're afraid it will make us look bad.

When you recruit up, you won't need to do the stuff they do!

The best way to build a great team is by recruiting up, by recruiting people who are better at what they do than you are. If you do this, you will build a great team. "Yes, but if I get people who are better than me, then they won't need me." No, if you get people who are better at doing some of this stuff than you are, you won't *need* to do the stuff they're doing. You won't need to follow them around all the time and make sure they're doing it. Leaders who recruit down never get a break. They always have to watch every move of their people. They are forced into micro-management. All their creativity is sucked out by the frustrations of managing an inferior team. They are doomed to high stress and low peace!

One precaution: If you're going to recruit up, you *must* run your team efficiently. Talented people do not want to step into a cesspool of frustration. If they see frustration and inefficiency in your team; if they see you doing everything the hard way; if they see you not working systems, then talented, sharp people will not work with you. And even if you do get them to come on board, they won't stay long. They will quit and create a real mess for you. So work your system and recruit up.

Two Sources for Leaders

A senior leader's dream is to develop workers who become leaders, who develop workers who become leaders, who develop workers who become leaders, and so on. In other words, *the law of multiplication!*

You are always looking for leaders.

If you are trying to build a multiple leadership team, you are always looking for leaders. Who are the "natural" leaders in the organization? Who are the ones who naturally inspire and influence others by their positive example? These are some of your potential leaders.

Leaders come from two sources: *internal* and *external*. Internal leaders are those who come up through the ranks whom you develop well. If you don't take people through the system, and they become leaders, they will destroy your system because they won't know what they are supposed to do. They won't know how to do it the way you want it done, and in the end it won't come out looking the way you want. It won't conform to your mission statement or your vision statement or any of the things that can make your organization great.

External leaders are people who are already successful, people who are already functioning at a higher level. These are talented, successful people you attract to your team but who did not come up through the ranks. As a leader, recruiting must always be on your mind just as much as doing a good job. Otherwise, attrition will erode your team and take away any success that you have achieved.

Essential Attributes for Recruiting and Team Building

Let's look now at some essential attributes for recruiting and team building. These are principles that we must understand as leaders if we hope to be successful in recruiting and building winning teams.

Leaders who only see people's weaknesses continually disqualify. I'm not talking about perfectionism here. If all you ever see are people's weaknesses, you will disqualify people. You will not motivate people, you will not develop people, you will not take them from where they are to a better level of performance. In fact, you will actually discourage them.

It's all right to notice what's wrong as long as you notice equally what is right. When you can see people's potential, you can look past where they are to where they can go. You can encourage them with their strengths instead of beat them down with their weaknesses.

You say, "What if I'm one of those people who tends to notice things?" Believe me, I understand! I am the "king" of noticing things. I can walk into any room, anywhere, in any situation, and it doesn't matter how much work you've put into it, if there is anything in there that is out of place, I'm going to notice it. It's not because I'm trying to be critical; it's because I have trained myself to do that. Years of construction work, years of organizing rooms for business use and years of having to pay attention have trained me to see what's wrong and fix it. I don't want to walk by something that's not the way it should be and fail to notice it.

Noticing and negativity do not have to go hand in hand. This means that when you notice something wrong you can do so without being negative or finding fault. It also means that you can now help bring quality to a situation by helping people understand how to bring something up to the level it needs to be. If noticing makes you negative, you are not ready for leadership.

Leaders who only see people's strengths are continually disappointed. If all you see are people's strengths, you set yourself up for a lot of disappointments. You become unrealistic in your expectations. You will have a tendency to trust people when they haven't been proven. All of us should want to see the best in people, but this doesn't mean you should close your eyes to their weaknesses and struggles. If you do and depend on them anyway, you will only end up frustrating yourself and them.

Leaders who understand people's strengths and weaknesses are never disappointed. When you understand the strengths and weaknesses of the people you are trying to recruit, you can avoid disappointment, frustration and failure by assigning them accordingly. Match a person's strength with a particular position that calls for that quality or skill. Match a person's weaknesses with a person who can mentor him or her.

Understanding people's weaknesses doesn't mean you place no value on them; it just means that you don't give them jobs in which you know they will fail. You don't put them in situations where you anticipate them not doing well. You're honest about their weaknesses, and it's even okay to talk to them about it, particularly if they start pushing to get into an area they're really not ready to handle. You can say, "I'll train you to go in this area, and I'll help you move in that direction, but I want you to understand that if you go into this area now, it will not work, and we do not want you to fail."

It's important, for your sake and for the sake of the team, to be honest about people's strengths and weaknesses. When people know you are honest about their strengths and weaknesses, your word will mean more to them. On the outrageously popular television show, *American Idol*, two of the judges, Randy Jackson and Paula Abdul, are pretty nice. They tend to compliment contestants even when they really don't deserve it. But Simon...he's the bad boy. He will tell contestants how bad they are and then some. As hard as he can be, people still value his compliments more than the other judges. They know that when he says it, it means something. They know that a compliment from a person who is honest really is a compliment.

Leaders who see people's strengths position properly. Once we recognize people's strengths, it becomes much easier to match them to a particular job description. When you do that, you can assure people they will probably succeed. This is so simple, yet so key. It is one of the eight critical factors of management. You always want to link people to the job.

One of the reasons we don't do this is because most "team builders" have a "whosoever will" policy. "Whosoever will sign up, we'll put you to work." This can be both good and bad. If somebody signs up, you want to find something for that person to do. Rather than matching a person's skill to a particular job, our normal tendency is to place someone in a spot even if we know he or she is not really suitable for it because we're desperate and need somebody to fill the position. Then he or she doesn't do well and you get frustrated. What's worse is that the person will be embarrassed and uncomfortable and may even get blown out of that team and perhaps even out of the church or whatever organization he or she has been working with.

Never hire "whosoever will."

If you have a business of your own, don't hire "whosoever will." You say, "Yeah, but I'm desperate. Right now I'm three weeks behind on my job." If you hire somebody who's not qualified, next week you'll be four weeks behind. He or she will make mistakes that you'll have to go behind and correct, and the whole thing will be a big mess.

No matter how desperate you feel, never recruit from a "whosoever will" mentality. It's better to leave a position unfilled than to fill it with the wrong person.

Leaders who see people's potential train properly. Once you see someone's potential, rather than just giving the person the job, find some way to train him (or her). Take him through the system to determine if you can depend on him to do the job. Don't just give somebody a job who hasn't been trained or proven. If you do, you will create trouble for yourself and the rest of the team.

Leaders who believe in the cause motivate. One of the main reasons you might be having trouble motivating your team is because you don't actually believe in the mission and vision statements of your team. If you do not connect to the value that your team brings to something, you will not be a team motivator. You may be a great worker or a pretty good organizer, but you will never be a strong motivator. If you believe in the cause, motivation should come naturally. It is only natural to be positive and excited about those things you believe in. On the other hand, if you do not or cannot believe in the mission and vision of the team, you need to step down as leader.

Leaders who work a system multiply. You cannot have multiplication unless you work a system. I cannot stress this enough. There is no other way to multiply. Systems are the only way to ensure things are done the same way every time. Systems give people a track to run on that ensures they will always reach the proper destination.

Leaders who connect with people recruit. Connecting is such a lost art. In the church world this is the ultimate secret to recruiting. If you are not actively involved with people, you will not be recruiting. I recently had a team leader who, like most leaders, said he was so busy he didn't have time to interact with the people. He and I had a frank discussion about how he would soon become frustrated from doing all the work. I talked to him about the importance of getting personally involved with the people.

"Well, what do I do? What do I say to them?" I replied, "It's simple. Just introduce yourself to people and ask them what they do. When they ask what you do, tell them what department you work in. The ones who are interested will express an interest. When they do, invite them to become involved." It all seemed too easy. He just couldn't believe it would work. So, I put one of my best recruiters with him and within two services he had five people interested in working on his team.

Recruiting happens out of personal involvement and influence. It doesn't happen because you make announcements or by any other impersonal technique. Recruiting only happens when you get personally involved with people.

The Lost Art of Leadership

Recruiting Begins in the Heart

Very often I will have somebody who is a really good person and a really hard worker who is leading a team that is dying from attrition. This person will tell me that he (or she) can't get anybody to help him. If I have the time, I can always recruit somebody. People always say, "But you're the pastor. People will always do it for you." There's a little bit of truth to that, but that is not really the key because I have found that I can take *anybody* who is a recruiter, put him in that situation, and he can get somebody to work on the team.

If you can't get anybody to serve on your team, you probably suffer from the same problem as Moses. After the exodus from Egypt, Moses was wearing himself out trying to minister to all the children of Israel. Like Moses, we get in that time trap; we're so busy doing things wrong we don't have time to stop and get it right. God told Moses to develop leaders and, interestingly enough, He told him to get a picture of leaders in his heart first. Exodus 18:21 reads like this:

> *Moreover you shall select from all the people able men, such as fear God, men of truth, hating covetousness; and place such over them to be rulers of thousands, rulers of hundreds, rulers of fifties, and rulers of tens* (Exodus 18:21).

The words *"shall select"* is the same Hebrew word that means to have a clear mental picture. It is the same word that is translated as "vision." God was not telling Moses to go out and find these guys. If Moses had the capacity to find the help he needed, he would have already found them!

That's the way it is when you're struggling with your team. It doesn't mean you're not a good person or not committed or not working hard. In one sense it's foolish of me to keep saying, "You need to recruit," because you're sitting there saying, "Yeah, I know I need to recruit, but nobody wants to help me; I don't know where to find them."

If that is your dilemma, then you may have the same problem Moses did. Moses' problem was heart. In his heart, he could not see people helping him. Before he could find people who would help, he had to have a vision in his heart. He had to have a clear mental picture that people wanted to serve and that people wanted to help. Once he could see it in his heart, he was able to identify them in the congregation.

Great recruiters are not more talented than anybody else. They're not more committed or more loyal or more spiritual. It's just that in this area of their lives they see, believe, understand and grasp the reality that people want to be involved. I assure you, your people *do* want to be involved.

Some years ago I took my entire staff through an exercise that opened everybody's eyes to the negative assumptions we make about ourselves and others. I asked them to visualize themselves sitting behind their desks with a stack of folders in front of them. The folders represented the projects for which they were responsible. Then I asked them to imagine different people coming in, talking for a few moments with them, then taking one of the folders and leaving. These people represented others who were accepting delegated responsibilities. Finally, someone comes in and takes the last folder. Their desks are now empty and clean. I then asked them to visualize me coming into their office and seeing them with an empty desk.

I asked them to tell how they felt when they gave away that last folder, when they saw their empty desk and when I walked in. In every instance, every one of them admitted to negative feelings. They felt guilty, uncomfortable; they felt that they had lost value and even that they had done something wrong. When I walked in they felt they had been *caught* doing something wrong.

At the heart level they could not see other people becoming workers and leaders and helping to carry the load. At that point, most of the team wanted me to hire people to assist them with their work. I would have been perfectly willing to do this if I thought more help would solve the problem. I told them, "If I hired people to help you, you wouldn't use them because you don't believe it's safe to *not* have something to do."

So often we value ourselves according not only to the work we do but also by how much of it we have to do. If we have nothing to do, we feel useless. Many times this obsession with work is an ego thing—we *need* to have too much to do because that is where we derive our sense of value. This goes back to the importance of having a healthy identity and self-worth that are not based on performance.

Wise leaders get satisfaction and fulfillment from having to look around for new things to do.

Wise leaders get satisfaction and fulfillment from having to look around for new things to do. It's an indication not only that they are getting the job done but also that they are involving other people to do it. We don't lose our value to the organization by not having anything to do; we lose our value when we won't let others help us.

Moses had the same problem. If you're beating yourself up because you just can't see it, remember that Moses became a leader who effectively led millions of people. And all that happened was, he saw it in his heart.

Recruit Only FAT People

Something I always tell leaders in training is that you only want to recruit "fat" people. "FAT" is an acronym for Faithful, Available and Teachable. We need to recruit people who are faithful, which means they should be *dependable*, *predictable* and *consistent*. Second, we should recruit people who are *available*. No talent is valuable unless it is available. Finally, we should look for people who are *teachable*. Good team members must be willing to learn and to work the system.

The first part of our acronym is *faithful*. I think we often misunderstand faithfulness. When I first got into building multi-level marketing teams, one of the first things I learned was, don't hire the "hotdogger." The hotdogger is the salesman who comes in and BOOM! Home run the first time up at the plate and BOOM! Home run the second time up at the plate. Now I'm counting on him—and he doesn't show up for work!

Faithfulness is not about people who from time to time do an exceptional job. We had a saying, "The hotdoggers will keep you from getting the good people." The super-performers will keep you from building a great team. If you build around your super-performers, a couple of things will happen.

First, the average person will look at the super-performer and say, "I can't do that," and will disqualify themselves. Secondly, you will find that super-performers never work the system. They make themselves the exception to the system, and so the system starts breaking down. If you start making allowances for them, before long no one else on the team will be willing to work the system either. Without the system, you cannot duplicate and multiply!

Faithfulness has to do with dependability and predictability. I have led all sorts of teams in all kinds of settings throughout my life, and I have learned that I would rather have an average producer who is predictable than a superstar who is not. Superstars are erratic; when they're hot they're hot and when they're not they're not! I can take that predictable person and after a year accomplish more than I could have with the superstar who tries to hit a home run every time. Usually with the "hotdoggers," it's all about them looking like a success and looking like a star. Their individuality is more important than the team.

Dependable, predictable, consistent. You have to have people who, if you say, "Be here at 9:00," will be there at 9:00, not 9:05 or 9:15. The hotdogger's attitude is, "I did so well the last time around that it should buy me some exemptions." The people who want to work from high point to high point think that those high points should buy them some privileges, but those privileges create an unmanageable situation and bring about a breakdown in the team. Get people who are dependable, predictable and consistent.

No talent or skill is valuable until it is available. It doesn't matter what a person can do if he or she is not willing to make it available in a predictable way, a way that you can manage or build something around or plan for the future or build a team. Over the years I have had many good people come around who had enough skill and would occasionally do enough work that I would depend on them, only to end up waiting. Then I could never create predictable schedules to work with them, and in the end they frustrated the entire process.

No talent or skill is valuable until it is available.

In any industry that depends on volunteers, availability is an indicator of priority. If what you are doing is a priority, people will schedule it into their life. Otherwise they will only give you the "leftovers" of their time. This person is not available. Even if their other priorities are legitimate, if they are not available this is not important enough to them.

Last of all, people must be teachable. Too often we think about teachable as only applying to the skill. I have found many people who will let you teach them concerning the skill they need to do the work, but they are not open to learning the system. You never know if a person is teachable until you start taking him (or her) through a system and see if he is willing to work the system with you. If he's not willing to work the system, he may be faithful and available but he's still not teachable and will still end up breaking down your system.

I have experienced an incredibly high number of people who, after creating chaos and conflict, finally admitted that they did not see the system as being that important. In the end I could not utilize their skill because they would not learn the system.

Every time, however, I have assumed a person's skill was good enough to justify breaking the system, I have always regretted it.

I have never seen a team built by people who would not work the system.

Beliefs and Attributes of Those Who Recruit and Build Teams

In closing, there are several basic principles or attributes that leaders who want to be effective recruiters and team builders need to understand.

People need to serve. We have to believe that people need to serve. Even people who are so incredibly loyal, so incredibly faithful, and who find a lot of personal fulfillment themselves in serving sometimes struggle with the idea that other people actually need to serve. Unless we recognize that people need to serve, we will not be inclined to ask them.

People want to serve. I believe people want to serve because I believe everybody has something inside that says, "I want to be significant." Whenever I walk into a room where things need to be done before an event, I'll start asking people to help here or assist over there. Some people might think this sounds bossy, but if so, they're missing the whole picture. I know that if people stand around and do not have the opportunity to contribute, they will start to feel insignificant and, before long, will leave feeling indignant and unappreciated. People almost always know *what* to do; they just don't trust themselves to do it. As leaders, we must not be hesitant to enlist their help. They really do want to be involved.

Have a kingdom vision. Another important belief and attribute for recruiters and team builders, particularly in churches and other ministries, is to have a kingdom vision. Not many believers—in fact, not many preachers—actually have a kingdom vision. A kingdom vision says, "I am a servant of the living God." If you haven't figured this out, I've got news for you: Your life isn't yours. We all have a purpose greater than ourselves. Romans 12:1 says,

I beseech you therefore, brethren, by the mercies of God, that you present your bodies a living sacrifice, holy, acceptable to God, which is your reasonable service.

A *living* sacrifice! Not a dead sacrifice or a spiritual sacrifice but a *living* sacrifice. It is reasonable for people who have been bought with a price to spend the rest of their lives serving God. If that does not seem reasonable to you, then you do not yet have a kingdom vision. You need to get a kingdom vision.

You have a purpose greater than yourself.

Even if you are building a business and not a church, the same basic principle applies. Your greatest success will come when you recognize that everything you do is for a purpose greater and larger than yourself and your own self-interest. As we saw in Chapter One, the most effective leaders are those who lead from the heart of a servant, and a servant's heart arises from an awareness that life and leadership are about more than just ourselves. Success comes when you give yourself to something and someone beyond the narrow scope of your own life and dreams and desires.

Another attribute you must have to be an effective recruiter and team builder is to *see the benefit it brings to people when they serve*. As a pastor I see it all the time. People come into the church and they do all the spiritual things they can think of, but it is not until they work in the parking lot or help clean up or help with some other activity that they discover that they finally feel a part of things. Why do they feel that way? Because now they *are* a part of things! Service yields genuine benefits in the hearts, minds and lives of those who serve. Don't deny them the opportunity.

Any effective recruiter and team builder will *be involved with people*. Each of us as leaders must be committed to becoming a people person on whatever level we can. This doesn't mean trying to become somebody we're not. Many people struggle with the idea of being involved with people. It simply means that we cannot let ourselves be content just to stay in our office and send memos. We must be approachable and available and willing to risk a certain amount of vulnerability. Getting involved with people is not always easy or comfortable, but we have no alternative if we want to recruit and build winning teams.

Finally, as recruiters and team builders we must be a "contactor" and a "connector." What's the difference? Contactors contact people. They make the initial contact. They can give you a good greeting. Making contact is important. The question is, do we then move to making connections? It will be in connecting that we will get people involved. This means that we have to become socially involved at some level with the people with whom we hope to build teams.

Continual recruitment is absolutely critical for building and sustaining winning teams and for creating an environment for ongoing success. Leaders who take the time to learn the principles and commit themselves to applying those principles have already won more than half the battle. Most of the trouble we have with recruitment comes from our own misconceptions, not from the lack of available, qualified and willing people. Learn the principles, set your intentions, get the vision clearly in front of you, and you will be surprised at how easy it is to recruit and build an unbeatable team!

Chapter Six

MULTIPLE LEADERSHIP TEAMS

❧❧❧

D eveloping leaders has changed dramatically in recent years. During my first 15 to 20 years in ministry I could often go into a church, find a person who had just become a Christian and in nine months release him as a well-trained, well-grounded leader.

In those days, society shared a common cultural and social understanding of life, work ethic and responsibility. Those were also the days when most households were single-income families. Because of this, leaders in training generally had more support from home or fewer responsibilities there. If the up-and-coming leader was a woman, she usually didn't work outside the home. Many of the essential factors for developing strong leaders was built into the fabric of society.

Much has changed since those days. Society has changed. Our culture has changed. Our economy has changed. Today there are very few single-income families. In most families, both partners work and sometimes one or the other or both hold more than one job. The demands and the mind-set of our society no longer provide a foundation for essential life skills, much less leadership skills.

Today the level of personal responsibility is very different from what it was then. In the 1960's and 70's you could take a drugged-out hippie or a drunk, get him clean and sober, lead him to Jesus and he would come into the church or re-enter the workforce with a greater sense of personal responsibility than many people have today. Many young adults entering the workforce today, including recent college graduates, MBAs and other advanced-degree recipients, have little or no practical work experience. A healthy work ethic is rare. In some cases, this is because they have had too many things given to them. More often than not, however, it is because no one ever taught them. Our children are growing up without models and mentors. Their education is of very limited value without the foundation of strong personal development through caring leaders.

Everything in our culture has changed. Today's average adult matures as much as 10 years later than in the 60's and 70's. Many of the traditional institutions of society, such as the family, have begun to break down. The deterioration of traditional moral values has set society adrift in a sea of moral relativism resulting in a significant rise of moral, spiritual and social chaos in people's lives. Most people walking into the doors of our churches today (or seeking jobs with our companies) have more personal chaos in their lives than people did in the 60's, 70's and 80's.

There are also more distractions today than ever before. You may have a leader or a worker who is doing great—learning, growing, maturing, producing—then, without warning, drop off the radar. A sudden crisis like sickness, death in the family, or financial reversal, and he drops the ball with little or no warning. It's not because he is incompetent or undependable but because the level of personal chaos in his life has become unmanageable, at least for the time being. This distraction renders him unable to concentrate sufficiently on his responsibilities. A senior leader who is not "in touch" may push for performance and blow the junior leader out or engender a terrible attitude.

As "new millennium" leaders, we cannot afford the insensitivity and ineffectiveness of idealism. Idealism sets unrealistic standards and expectations that actually lower productivity and longevity. We cannot accept the idealistic mantra of, "This is how it *ought* to be!" We must accept the real life logic of, "This is how it is." As innovative caring leaders, we must find a way to make healthy leadership principles and personal development goals and make them work in people's lives today.

As the needs and demands of society change we must adapt methodologies that create a win–win situation. Both the organization and the people must win. This never happens when your goal is to make things like they used to be or how they ought to be. In an ever-changing society we must find what works and adapt.

One of the best ways to develop strong leaders without overloading the *faithful few* is to develop *multiple leadership teams*.

A multiple leadership team incorporates the strengths and skills of a group rather than an individual. When leadership responsibilities are shared, the performance level rises as the stress level decreases.

The multiple leadership team approach provides several significant benefits to everyone. First, all the responsibility for the success of a team or department does not fall on the shoulders of one person. In a society that has lower standards of personal responsibility and a trend toward specializing, the idea of a shared load is very safe and appealing. No one has too much stress or too much control over the outcome.

Second, because of shared responsibility, everybody works less but accomplishes more. In other words, multiple leadership teams help provide maximum results for minimum effort. Third, multiple leadership teams mean that more people have a vested interest in the success of the team, the organization or the event. The probability for success in any given field increases with each leader.

On the other hand, leaders who do not build their teams and multiply leaders either burn out quickly or end up with an introverted team that does not grow. Growth is simply impossible when the leader or the team members feel saddled with the burden of trying to do everything by themselves. Innovative teams emerge in a pool of talent and fresh ideas. Every team leader contributes something unique to the goal. Everything I do as a leader is made better by each of my team members. They all bring unique insights, skills and solutions to every project.

Multiple leadership teams can relieve stress, reduce frustration, increase productivity, promote peace within the team, help build synchronicity and greatly increase the likelihood of success. What's even better is that multiple leadership teams can work in every area and at any level of the church, business or organization. There is no minimum size required either of the group or the task in order for the multiple leadership team approach to work.

The God Team

The concept of teamwork goes back to the very beginning of time—and before. According to the Bible, God Himself exists as a "team," a trinity of Father, Son and Holy Spirit. To accomplish His will on earth, each member of this "God Team" must do His part. Scripture lays out plainly very specific aspects of activity for each "team" member: Father, Son and Holy Spirit.

This teamwork concept is seen best in the life and ministry of Jesus. Jesus always worked in teams. He always sent His disciples out in teams of at least two. There is no indication in the New Testament that Jesus ever sent anyone out to do anything by himself. Jesus was committed to the team process because He understood the great innate power of teamwork.

For example, Jesus surrounded Himself with a team of 12 special disciples called apostles, whom He trained by instruction, modeling and mentoring. He also sent them out in pairs or other small groups to preach, teach and heal. His purpose was to prepare them to carry on His work after He was gone and to multiply leaders by training others as they had been trained.

A study of the lives of the 12 apostles reveals that the one apostle who failed was the one who was not connected in any significant way to anyone else on the team. Nearly all the apostles had either a close friend or a close relative functioning and serving with them on the same team. Judas was sort of the "odd man out." Had Judas been connected with someone else on the team to help him keep his perspective, he probably would not have made the compromises that led to his downfall.

Jesus always worked in teams.

According to the New Testament, after Jesus rose from the dead and returned to heaven, He gave gifts to the church for the purpose of continuing to build teams and develop people. Speaking of Jesus, the apostle Paul wrote:

> *And He Himself gave some to be apostles, some prophets, some evangelists, and some pastors and teachers, for the equipping of the saints for the work of ministry, for the edifying of the body of Christ* (Ephesians 4:11-12).

The offices of apostle, prophet, evangelist, pastor and teacher—known collectively as the fivefold ministry—exist for the purpose of "perfecting" (maturing, growing, training) the saints (Christians) for the work of the ministry and to "edify" (build up, develop) the body of Christ. Additionally, all kinds of ministry and serving gifts exist in the church, in the lives of individual believers. In short, all of this is a *plan* for *ongoing multple leadership development*. The church cannot become what it is called to be without the influence of a multiple leadership team. *Every member must do his or her part* starting with the leadership team and working through the entire body of Christ. The idea of one person being able to make it all happen is foreign to New Testament thought. In this sense, even the church itself is one big team.

Advantages of Multiple Leadership Teams

Multiple leadership teams provide a diversity of perspectives and strengths that make the overall efforts of every team member more valuable. As human beings, we are inclined by design for teamwork. We always function best when we work together with other people. Those who think they work well alone do not realize how much they limit themselves. They usually actually have a few areas where they function well and a few areas where they bottleneck. Several significant advantages come when people work in teams that simply are not there for people who try to go it alone.

First of all, leaders who work in teams experience higher productivity. At each stage of development a project must receive a specific type of input. The wrong input at the wrong time will halt a project in its track. Likewise, a project will develop much more quickly if it is handed off to a person with another set of skills at the appropriate time. Knowing when and to whom to pass the ball optimizes productivity and decreases conflict.

By passing a project to a leader with appropriate skills, great results are experienced at every stage of a project. They see the value their skill brings to the project without having the stress of leading in an area where they are weak. When people are weak in certain areas they tend to mismanage, neglect or overshoot in those areas, adding to frustration, high cost and low effectiveness. Very often great effectiveness in one area is lost in another when a project cannot be moved through the channels of a multiple leadership team.

Second, leaders experience less stress when they work in teams. Teamwork ensures that the burden for success or the responsibility for failure does not fall on the shoulders of one person but on the shoulders of everyone involved. Shared responsibility always relieves stress. Besides, a well-functioning team creates a positive environment that promotes high morale, fellowship and *esprit de corps*, all of which are stress-busters.

Leaders working in teams also accomplish more of the goals and objectives of the organization than do those who work alone. First of all, phases of the task can be divided and allotted across the team so that no one is overloaded. Each leader has time to prepare for his or her part as the project moves toward his or her area of expertise. Also, the work of the team can be divided according to the strengths and skills of each member so that no one gets bogged down and loses valuable time trying to perform work inconsistent with his or her skills. Teamwork ensures that the law of multiplication is in effect rather than the law of addition.

Leaders working as a team always have more fun than people who work solo.

Another benefit of working in multiple leadership teams is the mutual encouragement. Leaders working together toward a common goal develop a sense almost of kinship that promotes a spirit of encouragement, not only by word of mouth but also by assisting someone who's having trouble or by helping to work out a problem. Mutual encouragement is a powerful thing and can enable people in a group to do more and go farther than they ever could alone. Think back to the example of the migrating geese in Chapter One that honk occasionally to encourage each other on the long flight south and that never leave one of their own that falls by the wayside to fend for itself.

Leaders working as a team always have more fun than people who work solo. It's fun to succeed as a team because everyone is bolstered and lifted up by everybody else's pride and satisfaction at a job well done. It's said that shared joy is doubled (or tripled or quadrupled, etc.) while shared sorrow is halved.

Finally, leaders who work in teams encounter higher levels of consistent creativity. Creative, talented and diverse people working together inspire each other. When you work in a team situation, listening to others, receiving information from others, sharing ideas with others and brainstorming with others create an environment for a much higher level of creativity than when people work alone. The simple fact that different people think differently and come up with different ideas is enough to promote greater creativity among everyone.

The wisdom of Ecclesiastes 4:9-12 is very apt here:

> *Two are better than one, because they have a good return for their work: If one falls down, his friend can help him up. But pity the man who falls and has no one to help him up! Also, if two lie down together, they will keep warm. But how can one keep warm alone? Though one may be overpowered, two can defend themselves. A cord of three strands is not quickly broken* (Ecclesiastes 4:9-12 NIV).

Another scripture, Deuteronomy 32:30, speaks of one chasing a thousand and two putting ten thousand to flight. Notice that it doesn't say two putting *two thousand* to flight. There is an exponential power in play when people work in teams. Teamwork activates the law of multiplication, not addition. When people work in teams, the result is not *additional* productivity and creativity but *multiplied* productivity and creativity.

Hitler once said if he had 25 men who believed in his plan, he could take over the world. He never got 25 men, but he still almost took over the world. It does not take a lot of people to do incredible things. All it takes is a few passionate, committed people who work together and create synergy.

Then there is the safety net. If this project hits a stalemate, it can always be moved forward or back to a leader who has the skills that are essential to the moment! When things go bad, you are never alone!

No Secret Agendas

Teams are made up of people with different skills, strengths and weaknesses who hold clearly defined goals in common. When a group pursues a common goal, fellowship should begin to occur in the group, particularly if the leader helps create a social environment. Team members want to have fun with what they do and it is the leader's job to make fun a part of the work environment. People who enjoy what they do work harder.

A group may possess all the necessary skills, but if they are not pursuing a common goal they are not a team. One thing I learned playing high school football is you never want to run toward the wrong goal. A team is only a team when the members are pursuing the same goal.

People who enjoy what they do work harder.

Pursuing the wrong goal is one thing; pursuing multiple, conflicting goals is another. No team can function if its members are all running their own secret agendas or pursuing their own secret goals. Years ago I was preparing to bring a man onto our leadership team. He and I talked for months about what we wanted to do and how we were going to do it. When he finally came on board, in the very first week he violated many of the things we had talked about and agreed upon. When I addressed the problem I asked, "Didn't you understand what we talked about and agreed to and even put in writing?" He replied, "Yes, but I thought I could get you to do it differently." I said, "Well, you made a big mistake." And I had to let him go. You can't be on a team and pursue your own secret agenda. It doesn't matter who's right; conflicting goals destroy a team.

Don't hide a secret agenda. If you have an idea you think will work better, share it with the whole group. Good teams and successful organizations are always open to change if the change is beneficial. If for some reason you cannot agree with the identified goals of the team, you should remove yourself from the team. Anyone who pursues a secret agenda or a personal goal is not a team member. In fact, he or she is subversive, divisive and a harmful influence on the team.

The Bible asks: *"Can two walk together, unless they are agreed?"* (Amos 3:3) The obvious answer is *no*. Without agreement among every member of the team with regard to their common goal, team members will be working at cross-purposes. They will make little progress while creating massive conflict. But leaders who share a common purpose, values and goals become an unstoppable synergistic force that can accomplish anything.

The Character of Effective Leadership Teams

In addition to being highly skilled and focused on a common goal, there are several other qualities that characterize winning team leaders. As a matter of fact, these qualities could be said to define the *character* of effective teams.

Diversity is an essential *strength* for a team that consistently wins. The last thing we want is a group of people who are alike. And yet, that would be our natural tendency. We tend to recruit people who are like us. It is natural to look for similarity instead of diversity. We tend to be drawn to similarities for social more than professional reasons. Our natural affinity with like people gives us the often vain expectation of minimized conflict.

Two things can happen when we build leadership teams around similarities rather than diversity. We can have a great social environment. There may even be minimized conflict. However, productivity is usually very low. The workers win and the organization suffers. This is unacceptable. Remember, everyone must win for an option to be viable.

Then there is an often surprising revelation when we build around similarity. There are many people with whom we socialize very effectively yet we do not work well together. That which makes us compatible as friends does not always make us compatible as workers.

Leaders who think alike and who have the same strengths and weaknesses will tend to make the same mistakes. They share the same blind spots. Creativity experiences only a limited scope in similarity. Then, when things go wrong, conflict, tension and frustration will rise because no one saw the problems coming.

A leadership team should never consist of people whose most common denominator is they are buddies. As a leader, being friends with your team members is good, but just because you surround yourself with friends doesn't necessarily mean they can help you accomplish your goals. Sometimes all they'll do is help you find excuses when you don't.

Effective multiple leadership teams need a diverse mix of people. Diversity sparks creativity. Diversity stimulates creativity at each stage of development. Diverse people inject different ideas and points of view as they take a project through each stage. Just as a diversity of skills is necessary in an effective team, so is a diversity of personalities. When a group of people with different personalities and viewpoints come together to work, their discussions and exchanges can become very dynamic, injecting life, vigor, imagination, innovation and enormous creativity into the mix.

Effective multiple leadership teams need a diverse mix of people.

At the same time, leaders must build their diverse leadership teams very carefully. One place where there *must* be similarity is in shared values. Shared values create an amicable environment where everyone respects and values the differences. Otherwise, the very diversity that should bring incredible strength to the team will create conflict, thereby weakening the team.

Purpose is the second essential similarity in a multiple leadership team. Shared purpose brings shared *motivation*. If there is no shared purpose, we do not have the motivation to sustain us through the entire process. Each part of the development process stimulates every leader when he or she sees how each part contributes to the shared purpose.

As long as there is a clear-cut purpose and the leader keeps that purpose in front of the team at all times, team members will understand why they are doing what they are doing and how their job fits into the overall vision of the team or organization. For this reason it is valuable for the team to have regular conversations and discussions about their purpose and why they are doing the work they are doing. The "driver" personality struggles with the need for ongoing communication. Such people just want to do. In fact, they want to do without having to explain the whys. "Just trust me," seems to be their answer to every question. Thus, the other leaders, as well as the entire team, suffer from a lack of motivation.

Third, *values* are the *bond* that holds a team together. This is where great fellowship comes into the team. Do the team members value the things they are doing? Do they *see* the value their efforts bring to the rest of the team, organization or project? Do they value the benefit their efforts bring to the customers, clients or congregants?

Finally, *process* is the *lubricator* that keeps the team running smoothly. Everything else can be right—diversity, purpose, motivation and values—but unless everybody is in the same process and working the same system, there will be constant friction. Friction generates heat and can cause the mechanism to seize up and come to a sudden halt. Friction in a team due to lack of process will cause productivity to drop and frustration to rise.

Every behavior type has their own unique reason for avoiding systems. Their reasons make sense. But a failure to develop and live by a system that makes sense will stop the end results of mentoring and modeling...and multiplying.

Team Member Profiles

Multiple leadership teams built on diversity recognize the need of specific roles. It is the presence of these roles that ensure the highest levels of innovation. There are no hard and fast rules that say every team must have every role present to function; however, the more of these that *are* present, the more creativity and efficiency will flourish.

Perhaps the most important role on the team is the *facilitator*. A facilitator is a person whose primary strength is the ability to understand different people's points of view. From this insight, he or she helps each team member see and value others' viewpoints.

Let's say that a facilitator is sitting at the table with two other team members: a visionary-type and a "refiner" (the detail-oriented person). The visionary says, "Hey, I've got a great idea! Let's build a large boat and put two of every kind of animal inside!"

Immediately the detail person responds, "Wait a minute. Have you thought of how much food it will take to feed those animals or how big the boat will have to be? How much wood will we need and where will we get it? How much will it cost? How many people will it take? Do we have the necessary manpower, and are you expecting *me* to do this?" (This is the way most group meetings go!)

At this point, the facilitator speaks up. He says to the detail person, "Before you get too nervous, just remember that we will not attempt this without a plan. We won't just dive into this. We want input from everybody, so tell us what we need."

The detail person wipes his (or her) brow. "Whew! Okay, that's better. I thought we were going to jump right in and have this thing floating by Tuesday!"

At the same time, the visionary is upset at all the questions posed by the detail thinker. "You're killing my vision!" he insists.

"No," the facilitator answers, "these are simply the questions we must answer and the things we must do to make your vision come true. We just don't need to answer them at this point."

On any team, the facilitator is really the voice of reason and objectivity who helps everybody see that each one's viewpoint and contributions are valuable. The facilitator knows who needs the ball at any given time and is a master at the art of passing it from one to another at the appropriate time. There is a time when the visionary needs the ball in order to talk about the vision.

There is a time for the ball to go to the refiner to discuss the details, and so forth.

The problem that occurs without a facilitator is that everyone thinks now is the time for him or her to speak. They fear that if they don't speak now, their viewpoint will be overlooked and the project will suffer.

> *The facilitator is the key person who really makes a team work well.*

The facilitator is the key person who really makes a team work well. This does not mean necessarily that the facilitator is the person in charge. Even the team "leader" as such shouldn't always be in charge. Remember, a leader is not better than other team members. A leader is just a team member with different skills.

Team function is not about who is in charge as much as about each member stepping forward with his or her part at the appropriate time and having someone to help mesh it all together and move the work forward. The facilitator operates in this function, which is why every team needs one.

The second most important person/function on the team is the *secretary*. The secretary is the information person, the person who keeps track of all the different ideas and information generated by the team. When a team is operating in true synergy, or brainstorming together, visions, ideas, insights and information can be generated at a staggering pace. All this creativity is for nothing unless there is someone who makes records, organizes it, and tracks the information.

Some people really have a mind for this kind of thing and love doing it. It may not be glamorous work, but it is absolutely critical to the life, health and success of the team.

The secretary keeps track of all commitments, time lines and the follow-up information required to keep these on track. Every great leader and/or idea person will admit that one of their greatest weaknesses is follow-through. The secretary helps ensure that follow-through occurs by organizing all the ideas and information and reminding everybody at the appropriate time of what was said or what needs to be done at this point in time. Coming up with even the greatest plans and ideas is a waste of time without someone to manage the information.

A third essential role for an effective team is that of the *leader*. This is not a hierarchical title. As I said before, the leader is no more important than anyone else; he (or she) simply fulfills a different role. The key asset of a leader is his ability to always keep his eye on the ball. A leader always keeps the end in mind.

When I played high school football, my position on defense was safety, the deepest man on the field. My coach told me, "You have *one* job: *Never* lose the ball!" It didn't matter if the offense faked, made a lateral move, ran up the middle or passed; I had to keep my eye on that ball. If you're the deepest man on the field, you are the last stop before success or failure in every play. So is the role of the leader.

No matter what action is taking place, the leader keeps his eye on the ball. A leader is always able to look at what the team is doing and ask, "Is this moving us toward the goal?" As simple as this seems, it is an indispensable question. It is possible for teams to be busy, fulfilling seemingly important tasks that do not advance them toward the goal. The leader helps keep the team focused and on track.

Another important role is the *promoter/recruiter*. This person could also be called the "advancer" because he or she is the one who really wants to move things forward. The promoter/recruiter is the PR person, the person who likes to run with the plan. This person wants to move it forward now! In the example of building the boat and filling it with animals, while the visionary and the refiner are still discussing the idea to see if it's even feasible, the promoter/recruiter is calling everybody saying, "We're building an ark; it's going to be great! Come on out and bring a friend! Bring a hammer, too, and some nails!"

A PR person can sell something before it's even built. Their passion is to move the plan forward. If the PR is in charge, he or she will move ahead too rapidly with unfounded optimism, thereby creating pressure for the team to complete without quality. But the PR is essential. This individual promotes, recruits and sells the project. He or she is anxious to move it toward completion.

Every team also needs a *manager*, the person with the ability to organize the people on the team and help them understand their job. The manager is the one who organizes the work in such a way to ensure that all the necessary details are taken care of and that nothing is forgotten, ignored or left undone. Managers enforce the systems. In the ark example, the manager would make sure enough tools were available, would establish the work shifts, verify that the wood supplies are delivered on time and make sure everyone has everything needed so that there will be no idle time or idle workers.

Then there is the *planner/organizer*. This might be the refiner or detail person mentioned earlier. The planner/organizer is the one who identifies the specific details necessary for the plan to succeed: what kinds of tools are needed and how many; what kind of wood and in what lengths and quantity; the number of man-hours it will take to build the ark in a specific period of time; etc. Once the vision is established and the goal set, the planner/organizer goes to work setting up a plan to accomplish the task while avoiding chaos in the process.

Finally, every team needs a *minister*. For teams in a church or other ministry, the role of this person is obvious. The minister is responsible for the spiritual life and health of the team. In a business or other non-church setting, the equivalent function would be someone whose concern is the overall morale—the mental and emotional welfare of the team. The minister makes sure that the team is about more than just the work.

Sometimes in the heat of the work it is easy to lose perspective on the other, larger aspects of life. Our lives do not (or should not) revolve around our work. The minister helps everyone maintain a healthy life perspective. Many people who started out serving God lost their soul in the midst of the project. The minister serves the people to keep their lives balanced and their perspectives clear.

These are only a few of the possible roles or functions that people can perform within a team. The important thing to notice in all of this is the need for multiple leadership teams. The presence of each role adds to the development of people; the load is lightened, responsibility is shared and a vested interest is created through a shared ownership.

Churches and non-profit organizations that depend on volunteer help should master the multiple leadership team approach. In our current chaotic high-pressure society, people will more readily take a responsible role if they do not have to take all the responsibility. Plus when the leadership responsibilities are shared, the failure of one team member does not mean the total failure of the effort.

Chapter Seven

MODELING

❮❁❀❁❯

People believe and understand what they can see. Studies indicate that when there is conflict between verbal and non-verbal behavior, people always believe the non-verbal. The non-verbal is what we show; it is what people see through our expressions, gestures and actions. Regardless of what we say, our non-verbal behavior is what people will follow, duplicate and multiply.

Modeling is one of the most powerful and effective and yet most neglected training tools available. More than any other approach, modeling ensures accuracy. It almost completely removes the possibility of error. There is very little miscommunication in modeling. It is instruction come to life.

Through a combination of our western cultural mind-set, the industrial age and the now full-blown information age, our society has all but abandoned the time-honored, biblically based tradition of modeling. The sad result is visible all around us in a society of college graduates who really don't know how to make money, run a business or survive in real life.

From *The One Minute Manager* to *The Seven Habits of Highly Effective People*, a constant stream of wise and experienced voices have been calling us back to the leadership principles that work in real life. Modeling is one of the essential lost arts of leadership that must be restored. Our businesses, churches and, most importantly, our families will flourish when modeling becomes the primary mode of leadership.

Modeling requires much more from the leader than any other form of teaching. It says, "My life is a pattern you can follow. If you don't understand what I am trying to teach you, just do what I do and you'll get it." Our colleges are filled with men and women who have never succeeded at business. They can't make that promise. They haven't done what it takes to succeed, and they may not have seen it done. They just studied it! Our country is led by politicians, many of whom have never built a business or even held a real job. Religious leaders who have little experience in real life are continually frustrated in their attempts to help other people build their lives. Throughout all levels of our society there is a dearth of experienced people who can say, "Follow me!"

Modeling is character based. Because it requires proven experience it prevents the passing on of unproven theories and concepts. It makes both the teacher and the student true to the integrity of proven methods.

As crucial as it is, modeling is not a stand-alone modality. It is always most effective when combined with good information. If we must choose between instruction and modeling, modeling would be the most reliable way to ensure the accurate transmission of information. When joined, however, instruction and modeling together form the two essential concepts for making disciples and developing leaders.

Seeing Is Doing

For a number of years I had difficulty raising up "second generation" leaders. I had no problem developing first generation leaders, but they were rarely successful in developing the next generation. At first I blamed the leaders, but eventually I had to accept the obvious: Something in my leadership development plan was not congruent with my objectives. In time, I identified two specific weaknesses.

My first weakness lay in the fact that I had no absolute way of identifying and separating those who "walk the walk" from those who "talk the talk." Developing leaders is much like dating. When a guy wants a girl he can "fake it" for a long time before she finds out what he's really like. So it is with those who desire to be leaders. I knew there had to be a way of proving or testing those who expressed a desire to serve on my team without violating principles of integrity or pushing people into a performance mentality.

The second weakness of my system was that it did not provide a natural progression of development that started the day people walked through the doors and took them all the way through to finding a place to serve. My programs lacked congruence. My system was not a continuum but a set of various assorted programs. They all had the same goal but they did not flow from one stage to the other in a natural progression.

Discovering and adopting a more biblically based model of leadership development easily solved both problems. As I looked more closely at the biblical model I realized that I was using biblically based components but until then had not identified Jesus' process for bringing all the pieces together. Jesus modeled a pattern for developing leaders that included didactic training, modeling, supervision, teamwork, reporting, rewards and ongoing leadership development. All of these facets were components of a single system where each element formed a part of the continuum leading from belief to leadership.

Too often we try to develop leaders in a vacuum—the classroom. Anything can seem normal in isolation. Many theories look good on paper. They make sense in the theoretical realm but too often fail in the realm of real application. We evaluate students' knowledge for performing a task but we do not have a system that provides us with the opportunity to evaluate and develop their ability to apply what they have learned. We neglect their people skills. We fail to evaluate how they handle pressure. Furthermore, we have no way of really knowing the level of their commitment to our values. We have never seen how they resolve conflict. We don't even know if they really care about people.

Leaders cannot be developed in a vacuum.

Anyone can put the right answers on a test, but the real question is this: "Have they turned those answers into beliefs, attitudes and skills that work in a real-life setting?"

In our Bible college, we have had the opportunity over the years to observe and evaluate the difference between our correspondence students and our resident students. We have found that both groups can follow the same course of study, embrace the same theological positions, yet the correspondence students seldom truly grasp the spirit of our program. The correspondence students do not have the opportunity to sit in our church, observe our leaders and see how we apply the realities of servant leadership. They pass the tests and believe the same doctrines but in the absence of modeling they reach very different conclusions about application.

Let me give you an example. Years ago a student graduated from our correspondence program with the highest possible test scores. His written reports were excellent. When given the opportunity to work on our team, however, he failed miserably within just a few weeks. Our entire team was completely and utterly amazed. Upon analysis, we discovered that the primary factor in his failure was the absence of modeling. This student had received all his training through a correspondence program and consequently had never seen it work in real life. He had all the right information but had no capacity to apply our proven principles in a real-life setting. The one element missing from his training was modeling. This discovery resulted in a major shift in our hiring process. The result has been peace with productivity!

The absence of modeling doesn't just take away the students' opportunity to observe; it also takes away the teachers' opportunity to observe. When a teacher can observe the student in action, corrections can be made at the smallest level. Before an improper attitude or unworkable plan is put into action and becomes habit, it can be corrected. Huge problems can be solved before they have the opportunity to inflict sweeping damage.

Jesus and Modeling

If we want evidence of the value and time-honored nature of modeling as a leadership training tool, we need look nowhere other than the Bible. Modeling is the primary training method throughout the Bible, even more so than didactic instruction. The classroom lecture approach was much more prevalent among the Greeks. Modeling, however, was the preferred method for the Jews.

In the ancient Jewish traditions, spiritual leaders were rarely full-time professionals. Usually they were farmers, merchants or businesspeople. Their life was the validity of their message. In fact, it was impossible to separate their life from their message because their life *was* their message. If anyone doubted the efficacy of their teaching, they had simply to look at their lives to know whether their teaching was valid.

The greatest leader who ever lived, Jesus of Nazareth, the Messiah, did not stand in heaven and demand that people follow His orders. He became a man, lived among us and showed us how to live life to its fullest. His first invitation for training on His leadership team was very simple: "Follow Me!" He offered His followers the opportunity to see His teachings put into practice before deciding whether or not to accept a divine appointment. The model He lived was the proof of who He was and the process whereby He would develop His team.

Jesus had the perfect system for developing leaders. First, He taught the Word of God, which gave them the information they needed. Second—*and this is key*—He *modeled* what He taught. This, in my estimation, is the number one breakdown of leadership in our society today. We tell people what we want them to do but never show them how. Many of them won't even try out of fear of failing. Many who do try fail anyway, which discourages them from trying again. People fear the unknown. Until something is modeled, it remains an unknown.

Until something is modeled, it remains an unknown.

Although the word *modeling* is found nowhere in the Bible, it was nevertheless Jesus' ultimate training tool for helping man understand God. Since the time of Adam, man has studied God. Like all objective research, however, conjured in a heart veiled by sin issues, man's view of God is always slanted to facilitate personal prejudice, justify disobedience and protect us from our fears. By the time of Jesus, the religious leaders had so lost any accurate understanding of God that they had separated themselves from the people and become religious "professionals." The situation was so bad that God had to come in the flesh to accurately reveal His nature.

In the tradition of the pagan world, the religious leaders withdrew from the world and debated the abstract concepts of doctrine. Right was proven by who won the argument. The religious world had become a political system that violated its most core concepts as a way of proving itself right. As the apostle Paul so transparently confessed, he persecuted the church; he put innocent people in prison; he consented to murder. In the religious system as it had evolved, not only was he blameless, he was promoted and honored.

God didn't stay in heaven and say to mankind, "Understand this." No, Jesus became a man and said, "Watch what I do; observe how I treat people." We had to see God in the flesh before we could free ourselves from the stifling religious traditions that had been created apart from an honest model. We never know what we know until we see it done.

Jesus modeled the principles of life as well as the principles of ministry. He modeled the reality that everyone was important to Him. Even after the disciples heard His teaching about the kingdom of God, they still would have turned little children away so they wouldn't "bother the Master." Then they *saw* Him take the time to minister to the children, and they began to learn: "Oh, this is important." Even after they heard Him proclaim healing for all, they tried to silence a blind man who cried out for that very thing. Then they *saw* Him take the time to answer the man's appeal, and they learned a little more. They heard the message that the people of God are servants, but until they *saw* Him demonstrate it by washing their feet, they did not learn what it really meant. They had to *see* servanthood in action before they could develop the heart of a servant. Jesus continually modeled what He taught. This may be the single most important factor for understanding the effectiveness of the early church—they saw it put into practice!

It is in modeling that we *see* realities.

After Jesus allowed His disciples to see Him implement the Word, He gave them opportunities to minister. Many times they failed, which is only normal for learners. Jesus then gave instructions and modeled the solution. People today need to be observed and receive immediate and relevant feedback about their performance. While it is still fresh on their minds, they need to be able to ask the questions that the situation presented to them.

Next, as we saw in the previous chapter, He sent them out in teams to minister together. Now they had the opportunity to go out on their own and put it all into practice. In this setting, they would correct their own mistakes. They would learn to listen to God for themselves. But they were not alone. They had someone with them. Although the Scriptures do not say, I assume that one in each pair may always have been more experienced than the other. People are stronger and more confident when ministering or working in teams. They are also much more apt to follow the plan when they have emotional support and accountability.

After working and ministering in pairs for a while, the disciples came back and reported to Jesus all that had transpired. It was a time of reward and acknowledgment. Sharing experiences and testimonies is always a healthy part of development. It is also a great opportunity for further development. People receive instruction not only from the teacher but also from their peers.

The disciples then continued with Jesus. As they observed Him, they fine-tuned their own methods. None of us really knows which questions to ask or what to look for until we have had personal experience. I have found this to be true in our Bible college. Many of our students already have years of ministry experience while some are fresh out of high school. A tremendous gap exists between the types of questions asked by the two groups. Those with experience ask relevant questions. Their experience guides their learning process. The ones who have no experience do not yet know what they should ask. Training *after* experience is where the true skills are developed. This is the point at which people know what to look for and what questions to ask.

Whenever I read the New Testament, I am always amazed that the church survived its first decade. Jesus spent a little more than three years with a group of 12 men, all of whom had personal problems. They fought among themselves. They struggled for power and position. Jesus Himself rebuked them more than once for unbelief and hardness of heart. Yet, 2,000 years later, the church is here. The seed that Jesus planted was not lost through inept leaders. Despite their personal problems that continued until their deaths, they fulfilled their call.

Paul and Modeling

Another great New Testament example of leadership by modeling is the apostle Paul. In the book of Acts we are told that Paul went into an area, won people to Christ, taught and developed them, planted churches, ordained leaders for those churches and then left. Somehow, these novices successfully assumed great responsibilities. This is unheard of in our generation. If we left a new church in the hands of new converts today it would be disastrous. Yet, out of these seemingly impossible scenarios, powerful churches arose that endured and influenced the world for centuries.

Paul's success in raising up leaders started with selecting qualified people. Like Jesus, Paul taught them the Word. But over a prolonged period of time, he also modeled how they should live and function. He was so committed to the power of modeling that he said in 1 Corinthians 4:16, *"Therefore I urge you, imitate me."* This was not an egotistical boast but a commit-

> *Healthy modeling was a key ingredient in the success of the early church.*

ment to a lifestyle. His ministry was his life. And his life was his ministry! They saw how he handled people, pressure, success and failure. Before the New Testament was penned, the leader's life was the Bible people read to understand Jesus. Toward the end of his life, Paul wrote this to Timothy:

> *But you have carefully followed my doctrine, manner of life, purpose, faith, longsuffering, love, perseverance, persecutions, afflictions, which happened to me at Antioch, at Iconium, at Lystra — what persecutions I endured. And out of them all the Lord delivered me* (2 Timothy 3:10-11).

Timothy had seen it all. He had traveled with Paul. In those areas where Paul did not have a person to leave in charge, he often stayed for as long as two years. Healthy modeling was a key ingredient in the success of the early church. Often Paul left someone in charge who had been developed through the modeling process. This element is conspicuously absent from our present-day mentality. We take the potential leader into a classroom, teach him (or her) a few lessons with no personal involvement and expect him to go out and succeed as a leader. Then we are surprised and upset when he fails.

Paul modeled the principles of leadership to Timothy and encouraged Timothy to continue in that same method of teaching. Timothy faced many difficulties in his ministry. Paul never told him to use his authority as the way to solve a problem; nor did he tell him to rely on teaching alone. Instead, Paul told Timothy to teach and model the truth:

> *Don't let anyone look down on you because you are young, but* **set an example** *for the believers in speech, in life, in love, in faith and in purity* (1 Timothy 4:12 NIV, emphasis added).

Paul gave similar instructions to Titus, another young protégé:

> *Similarly, encourage the young men to be self-controlled. In everything* **set them an example** *by doing what is good. In your teaching show integrity, seriousness and soundness of speech that cannot be condemned, so that those who oppose you may be ashamed because they have nothing bad to say about us* (Titus 2:6-8 NIV, emphasis added).

Paul saw the life of Christ as a place to see the Christian life modeled. The mercy of God was taught in the Old Testament, but the people never comprehended it. When Isaiah said, *"My thoughts are not your thoughts, nor are your ways My ways"* (Isaiah 55:8), he was specifically referring to God's complete mercy for the sinner. The Jews never saw the mercy. Jesus came as a man and modeled the realities of God's character. When Jesus modeled mercy for tax collectors, sinners and the woman caught in adultery, He was reviled. The character of God was foreign to the people because they had never seen it before. Paul said that God's mercy on him should serve as a model for the entire church world.

> *Here is a trustworthy saying that deserves full acceptance: Christ Jesus came into the world to save sinners—of whom I am the worst. But for that very reason I was shown mercy so that in me, the worst of sinners, Christ Jesus might display his unlimited patience as an example for those who would believe on him and receive eternal life* (1 Timothy 1:15-16 NIV).

Paul was not an egomaniac. He was simply a committed Christian. By no means did he do everything right, but he always sought to live and model the life of a believer so that others could learn and grow also. To the Philippians he said, *"Join with others in following my example, brothers, and take note of those who live according to the pattern we gave you"* (Philippians 3:17 NIV), and to the Corinthian believers he wrote, *"Follow my example, as I follow the example of Christ"* (1 Corinthians 10:33 NIV).

Like the ancient Jewish spiritual leaders before him, Paul learned the secret that his life *was* his message. There was no difference between the two. He did not believe and speak one way and live another. His ministry was a continuum of his life. Paul's life had congruency in speech and behavior. He was a master modeler. Everything in his life and ministry said, "Follow me!"

The Leader and Modeling

As I said earlier, when our verbal and non-verbal communications disagree, the non-verbal is what people believe. Actions really do speak louder than words. How we handle people, how we act under pressure, what we do when we are angry; all of these communicate volumes of information to those who observe. What we *do* in a situation reveals what we really believe, regardless of what we say. People get to know us by watching our behavior. After that, it doesn't matter what we say.

Western culture may be the only culture in the world that places no value on the apprenticeship program. We see the consequences of this in the lives of our young people today. Mentoring is a lost concept. We are information mongers. Our answer for every problem is to gather more information. We fail to understand the dynamics of the human process. Fathers do not model for their children. Few companies still have apprenticeship programs. We have higher education, which produces young people with a head full of knowledge but no wisdom. The man with the degree gets ahead even if he has no life experience. Even when his abilities do not match his degree, he is the one who gets the promotion. Our culture encourages the development of foolishness. All the while a common cry from the corporate world to the pulpit is the fact that leaders don't really know much about making things work in a real-life setting.

In our attempt to communicate, we are always working through the other person's paradigms. They interpret everything we say in light of their personal, predetermined concepts. This means that there is often a huge gap between what we are saying and what they think we are saying. Even when the concepts are properly understood there is still a problem in understanding the application. All of these problems are effectively eradicated through modeling. Teach a man what to do, and he may forget. Show a man what to do, then let him do it, and he will get it right—today and every day.

Show a man what to do, then let him do it, and he will get it right.

As leaders, we should never teach anything in our leadership development process that is not modeled. This sometimes makes the difference between leaders and managers. We should not manage people but lead them. We *manage* time and resources, but we *lead* people. Management is about taking control. We should take control of ourselves, our time and our resources. We should plan and use our time and resources to fulfill our personal agendas. But we should never use people; we should lead people. Modeling is the first step in leading people. It establishes a never-ending cycle that initiates and develops a bond between teachers and students. It is the first key to multiplication!

Leadership is simply walking ahead of people. As leaders, we create the path for others to follow. We demonstrate how it is done. We make followers feel safe and secure in the pathway. We do not simply point people in a direction; we lead them in that direction. Moses did not stand at the Red Sea and say, "Go that way." He led the Israelites across on dry land. Just as those people needed to feel safe about walking in the midst of the sea, we must make our co-leaders feel safe about where they are asked to walk. We need to show them the safety in being servants. This concept is so foreign to the natural mind that it is inconceivable. We must model every step of this process.

The Distant Leader

Although it is only natural that we all give more time to certain people than to others, great leaders are never far removed from the people. Jay Abraham, a renowned consultant, asks the critical question, "How involved are you with the transactions that take place in your business? How far removed are you from where the real business happens?"[1] Maybe this was the secret of the success of the wealthiest man in America, Sam Walton, who regularly appeared at local Wal-Mart stores to greet guests and to observe.

> *Great leaders are never far removed from the people.*

It seems that too often the most productive people in our leadership teams end up isolated in an office, buried under mountains of paperwork where they can no longer influence their teammates with their incredible example. Instead, people far less effective are given the most influential jobs of developing and leading the team on a personal level.

The moment we isolate ourselves in an office and take on the role of paper shuffler, a breakdown begins in our business, ministry or family. It stops becoming what we envision it to be and begins to take on the characteristics of those who have more direct influence. Such isolation of leadership helps explain the current downward trend of many organizations and often spurs the onset of reduced productivity and compromised goals.

Many would-be leaders tend to shy away from modeling for a variety of reason. The greatest of these may be the personal demands of integrity. Modeling requires a high degree of visibility and a willingness to get close to the people. Many modern managers find either prospect frightening. Hiding behind a closed office door doesn't require much in the way of ethics or integrity.

Many leaders are afraid of the time investment. In the beginning modeling costs more. It is a huge investment in time and money. It is not a quick fix! But like all wise investments, it reaps dividends far greater than the original cost. Modeling gets long-term predictable results unattainable from any other methodology.

A commitment to the value and process of modeling is missing in the leadership development programs of most organizations. As we have seen, Jesus and Paul relied heavily on modeling to develop potential leaders. Modeling is all but impossible in an environment that says leaders should not be too close to the people. The idea is completely cross-cultural.

This idea of distance is what sustains the false elevation of a leader above the people. In the church, this idea has perpetuated the clergy-laity hierarchy. In business it is seen in labor-management dichotomy. It is evident in the leadership style where policies and pronouncements come down from on high with little or no interaction or input from the workforce. Such an approach puts a leader on a pedestal that isolates him so that the people cannot as easily see his flaws and frailties. In the end, it always backfires because the pedestal creates unrealistic expectations of the leader in the minds of the followers. The inevitable fall or exposure of the leader as someone no better or higher than anyone else creates disillusionment and frustration.

A distant leader cannot experience the incredible power of modeling. Through his lack of personal interaction, his own leadership skills begin to diminish. He or she loses the "pulse" of the people. In time, the out-of-touch leader is a dinosaur. If modeling is going to work, a leader must be visible, available and approachable.

The Approachable Leader

One of the greatest things you can do to win the affection and commitment of your people is to be an approachable leader. The approachable leader doesn't have much chaos in his or her ministry or business. These leaders usually discover problems when they are small and easily resolved. They have the respect, trust and love of the people. But most of all, they make people feel safe! Remove the cloud of darkness by making it safe for people to approach you. You won't believe the results!

An unapproachable leader is always in the dark. He or she never really knows what is going on. Usually there are lots of surprises and no lack of conflict. To avoid unwanted surprises and minimize conflict we must be in touch with the people. *We* must make it safe for them to talk to us.

However, nothing takes us by surprise as much as when people feel safe enough to tell us the truth. We want the truth, but it makes us mad if it is not "the truth" we want to hear. But we have to choose one or the other because we can't have both. The truth we *need* to hear may not be the truth we *want* to hear!

Our modeling openness, transparency and approachability will do more good than a year of sermons or a thousand memos.

I regularly tell my people, "You can say anything you want to say to me. You can question anything I do. Just be kind!" Most conflicts thrive because of the absence of communication. As leaders, we have a great opportunity to teach people how they should communicate. Being approachable, therefore, becomes a great instructional tool. Our modeling openness, transparency and approachability will do more good than a year of sermons or a thousand memos. When we are approachable, the people become approachable.

When people don't feel safe approaching us, they tend to store it all up. When it does come out, it usually comes out as an attack. Then, because it is said in an inappropriate manner, we reject vital information that could save us future conflict.

It is a frightening thing for most people to overcome their feelings of insecurity and to say anything challenging to a leader. In many circles people are not allowed to challenge or question their leaders. When this is the case, people hold it all in until they are angry. Then it comes out in uncontrollable, unacceptable torrents that can destroy relationships or cost jobs. Unfortunately, we sometimes use their weakness to justify our closed response, and the syndrome simply grows. When they can't talk to us, they talk to everyone else. The workplace becomes a hotbed as tension and frustration rise. Everyone is affected.

When people approach me and seem to be losing control, I usually stop them and say something like, "You know that I am willing to talk to you. I am really interested in what you have to say. But if you are going to attack me, or say it in a destructive manner, we won't make any real progress. Wait until you calm down and then let's talk about this. If you have a complaint and I need to deal with it, I will. But it will be hard for me to deal with it reasonably if I feel attacked."

Most of the time they calm down. It is usually their fear of confrontation that gets them all worked up in the first place. By my being reasonable and approachable, those who want and need a healthy conversation are able to have one.

This makes an incredible difference in the area of ownership. People will not take ownership if they are not able to disagree with us, challenge us and make a lot of their own decisions. If they do not feel safe, they will be so afraid of doing something wrong that they will do very little and initiate nearly nothing. In environments where leaders are unapproachable, one common complaint is that the people don't take initiative. In the biblical parable of the talents, it was one servant's fear of his master that led him to bury the money he had been given and do nothing rather than take the initiative to invest it. Productive people need to feel they can safely approach their leaders.

Maybe this concept of being approachable is new to you and you feel nervous or uncomfortable. You may even feel like you are making yourself *too* vulnerable. Perhaps you are afraid of what people really will say to you. And, for a while, you may hear some of the negative things that people have been storing up. But in the end, as you become more transparent and vulnerable, they will too. Becoming approachable is an incredible journey to growth and development for everyone.

Ten Practical Steps to Approachability

Here are ten practical steps to consider when working to become a more approachable leader.

1. Make yourself accessible. There may be nothing that makes you appear more unapproachable than the lack of presence. We all have busy schedules, but we must find ways to be visible. A few minutes greeting or talking to people after a church service or during a break or during the lunch hour has incredible influence. Participating in a social function can go a long way toward changing your image. Sometimes image is the whole problem.

2. Treat people like friends. Jesus told His disciples they were His friends (see John 15:15). Few leaders know how to be friends with their people and still be the leader. This dichotomy is an illusion that arises from unscriptural and unsound concepts of leadership. One of the most common characteristics of friendship is conversation. Become conversational. Remove the mystique! One of the marks of real friendship is openness.

3. Always express value for people's points of view. An approachable leader conveys value for the opinions of others. Even when you disagree with the opinion, people appreciate the opportunity to share. It makes them feel important. Sometimes it is more important that you hear them than it is that you agree with them.

4. Stimulates ownership. If we want people to own, be responsible and committed in their roles, they must feel they can discuss anything about their tasks or their life. If you are unapproachable and unrelenting in your point of view, they will see it as your ministry, your project...yours, yours, yours! They see themselves as little more than slaves who are paid to do your bidding. With that kind of attitude, they will never become the proactive initiators that you desire them to be.

5. Eliminate judgment. When it is safe to ask, there is no need to assume. People need to be able to ask questions. They need to have legitimate answers. A leader creates a safe place for him or herself to be real by allowing people to ask questions. This eliminates the tendency toward suspicion and judgment.

6. Never defend. When we do not let people say what they need to say, we appear defensive. When we make excuses, it appears that we are defending ourselves. The best response to an accusation is, "I didn't mean to hurt you, please forgive me." If the accusations are false, then the next question should be, "Can we discuss any of this?"

7. Seek to understand. In his incredible book *The Seven Habits of Highly Effective People*, Stephen Covey gives this advice, "Always seek to understand before seeking to be understood."[2] When people realize that you want to understand their point of view, they let their defenses down. They open their heart to you. When you seek to be understood, you come across as argumentative and disinterested in their point of view. They become closed and defensive.

8. Don't hide behind the Scriptures or "company policy." Preachers are the world's worst about hiding behind the Scriptures—as if we hold some privileged position that puts us above being questioned. We, more than anyone else, should allow people to question and challenge us. The same is true for the business or corporate leader who shields him or herself from questions or criticism by simply saying, "That's the way it is." No leader is above question, and an approachable leader will not try to be.

9. Encourage and reward creativity. People who feel safe experience the emotional freedom to be creative. They think outside the box. They introduce ideas. They give us input and suggestions. They make all our ideas better. They find this freedom because they are not consumed with the need to protect the ego of their leaders.

10. Sow what you want to reap. Make sure that the way you are treating people and communicating with them is what you want them to do in your life. According to James 3:1, we who are leaders receive a much stricter judgment, not from God but from people. Be open and they will be open. Confess your faults and they will confess theirs. Own your issues and they will own theirs. Treat people the way you want to be treated.

Delayed Gratification

Modeling requires a lot of up-front investment. It is a form of delayed gratification because many of the greater benefits and results do not appear right away. Before long, however, modeling gives us not only the freedom we desire but also the assurance that the job will be done the way we want it done. Effective modeling never costs; it *always* pays. It just doesn't pay *today*!

Endnotes

1. Jay Abraham, Audio Seminar, "How to get from where you are to where you want to go" (Niles, Illinois: Nightengale-Conant Corporation, 1997), Tape 1.

2. Stephen R. Covey, *The Seven Habits of Highly Effective People: Restoring the Character Ethic* (New York: Simon & Schuster, 1989).

Chapter Eight

MENTORING

❦

The commitment to develop people is sometimes frightening. Our faulty paradigm of leadership conjures in our minds fearful images of endless hours spent teaching people to do what they should already know how to do. The idea of investing in others often gives rise to the deceitful attitude, "It would be easier to do it myself!"

That's true. It *is* always easier to do it ourselves...in the beginning. Eventually, however, a leader who works from this philosophy will end up worn out and *attitudinal* from trying to do everything. This same philosophy feeds a leader's drive to micro-manage. The micro-manager may not believe his team is trained well enough to do the job without his constant supervision. Or he may not trust their work ethic to do the job on their own.

Both of these scenarios often stem from the fact that a leader has not made the right investments in his or her people. As we saw with modeling, effective leaders need to be available and approachable. Team members and employees need to know they can come to their leader with questions, problems, ideas or insights and be received in a positive manner. They also need to have the confidence of knowing that their leader cares enough about them personally and professionally to ensure they have everything they need to do their jobs well. And without question, they must receive sufficient training for every task.

By the time we as leaders reach any serious level of success, it often seems impossible to take the time to train people. We're too busy. We have too many important deadlines to meet. Training will have to wait because we've got to get the work out. Such an attitude is a deadly trap sustained by a deceitful illusion. When a leader is too busy to train people, he or she is too busy. This is a signal of a desperate need to change the current leadership paradigm. It is time to try something different.

People rarely have everything we want when we hire them. Even if they already possess the necessary job skills, they still know nothing of our policies, procedures and philosophies. Every organization has its own culture, its own way of functioning and relating to people. Culture relates to the emotional factor involved with the question, "How do things work around here?" In many situations, violations of culture create more interpersonal chaos than violations of procedure. If we don't establish our people in our policies, procedures and philosophies, they will create their own. This is how office politics emerge.

Great companies have great orientations and great training programs. These may be costly to initiate and operate, but those costs are more than compensated for by greater productivity, success and workplace harmony down the line. Orientation and training programs are not expenses as much as they are investments in the future of the company and in the lives of the people who make it work.

With the incredible resources made available to us today we need not always spend tens of thousands of dollars training our people. I have often reaped incredible benefits from a $49 investment in a training video. In-house training, peer-to-peer training and, most importantly, mentoring are resources that are within the reach of every business or ministry.

The people we hire will believe their job is only as important as the training we give them. Absence of training communicates certain negative messages by default: "Your job is not that important" or (and this is a real killer) "We expect you to know everything so don't ask questions" or (in keeping with the great independent American spirit) "I'll just do it my way." Perhaps the greatest lack in today's workforce is the absence of a plan for developing people. The resulting inefficiency creates an endless list of problems. An effective mentoring program is the only solution.

A mentor is a trusted counselor, guide, tutor or coach. The word comes to us from the Greek, specifically from Homer's *The Odyssey* where "Mentor" was a friend of Odysseus who was entrusted with the education of Odysseus' son Telemachus. The act of mentoring in the Scriptures is called discipleship. In today's substance abuse programs, sponsors mentor new participants in the way the program works. The concept of a mentor as a teacher in an intimate one-on-one relationship with a student has been presented from many sources.

In today's business and ministry environment, mentoring can occur on several different levels. Corporate mentoring often occurs through didactic teaching programs. These are essential because without them, endless hours are wasted answering the same questions over and over. After only a brief period of existence, every organization should know the questions that need to be answered at the onset of the relationship. These should be addressed through the orientation.

Every new employee, staff person, manager or leader, no matter what level, should go through a systematic and well-established process of corporate mentoring. This will help ensure that everyone in the organization understands the purpose, philosophies, goals, objectives, policies and procedures of the organization. This facilitates good communication and lessens misunderstandings, therefore reducing workplace confusion, frustration and friction and freeing everyone to produce more with greater satisfaction and efficiency.

A good corporate mentoring program lays the foundation for individual mentoring.

Mentoring Begins With the Pre-Hiring Process

No one, either leaders/supervisors or potential workers/staffers, wants to get into an inappropriate or unworkable relationship. This is why a clear, well-developed pre-hiring process is very important. Among other things, a healthy pre-hiring process provides the opportunity to present the potential staff member or volunteer with the "deal breakers." Deal breakers are those things that say, "We don't need to be working together." If the deal breakers are known during the hiring process, they should be thrown into the mix early. It's not good to begin the costly journey of integrating a new team member only to have that member blown out by the deal breakers.

If you hire the right people, mentoring becomes more a matter of coaching than teaching. The only way to know if you are hiring the right person is through the hiring process. The hiring process is the front door, the place and the manner by which people come into your organization. If you have a great front door, you'll have a great back door. If you hire slowly, taking people through a meaningful process, you will find the "right" people, increase effectiveness and minimize turnover.

Ted Nicholas points out in his course *Magic Words* that a leader should be slow to hire and quick to fire. At first glance this might seem a little cruel, but it is not nearly as cruel as hiring too fast and waiting too long to fire. The latter promotes much more pain and suffering. An impatient leader always hires too quickly. The need to gratify his impulsiveness forces him to justify swift, often premature, decision-making. Sometimes he or she is under pressure from upper management to fill positions quickly. Either way, rapid hiring does a great injustice to the organization, the current staff and the new employee.

The leader who hires too quickly will always regret it. Some organizations do not have the opportunity to observe a person in a non-paid role before hiring him or her. Because of lawsuits honest work references are hard to obtain. In such cases, those charged with the hiring process should find out all they can. Too often in such a situation a leader will make a hiring decision based on personal affinity, a hunch or an intuition: "I just feel good about this person." I'm sorry, but that is insufficient grounds upon which to justify a professional decision that will affect this person's livelihood and perhaps even the stability of the

The leader who hires too quickly will always regret it.

entire organization. Even if you have a good track record for making decisions in this manner, it is always safer and better to confirm with hard evidence before making a commitment. After all, we are dealing with people's lives and futures, and we must handle them with care.

Too often we hire like we date. In dating we are afraid to let our potential spouse see any of our negative traits out of fear that he or she will no longer like or desire us. The real pain, however, comes *after* the marriage when all of those traits come out and end up destroying the relationship. It is always better for the organization and a potential employee or staff person to learn upfront the good and bad on both sides before either side makes a commitment. This helps minimize the chance of a bad "marriage." There are plenty of good, talented, skilled, motivated people who may simply not be suited for your particular team or group. The best time to find that out is before an applicant becomes an employee. A healthy pre-hiring process helps make that determination in a way that preserves the dignity and worth of both sides. It avoids a lot of heartache, regret and financial loss.

Another important part of the pre-hiring process is to check the potential employee's employment record, credit history and every other available bit of information. This is not to be nosy or to learn things that can later be used to control somebody, but to identify trends of behavior or elements of the person's personal life or situation that will affect their performance in the workplace. Unless a moral or ethical problem is revealed, none of these single bits of information by themselves should qualify or disqualify a person. It is a way for a leader to understand and become sensitive to the external factors in people's lives that will affect their attitude and performance in the workplace. Sometimes it helps identify potential future trouble spots.

Obviously, such a careful approach to the hiring process means that the length of time involved in bringing a new person on could be quite long. That's okay. There is a natural safety in hiring slow. Many mistakes occur because decisions are made out of expediency. A careful and systematic pre-hiring process keeps us from hiring quickly just to fill a need. As I've said before, it is better to leave a position unfilled than to fill it with the wrong person. A temp is always a better decision than a guess!

Good teams are built around longevity, relationship and personal commitment. But it takes time to build this kind of team. It is well worth the time and effort to make sure beforehand that a new person will be a "good fit" for the organization. A slow hiring process helps avoid unpleasant surprises. We should always hire with integrity, never losing sight of the fact that we are dealing with people's lives and livelihoods.

A Personal Example

As an example of how such a pre-hiring process can work, let me share with you how we do this at Impact. In a ministry situation it is particularly important to know all you can about a person before making him or her a part of your ministry team. At Impact we use a behavioral profile that helps us understand how a potential ministry team member may relate to others. What motivates and de-motivates this person? How does this person respond to stress? How does this person communicate? How flexible and adaptable is this person? How does this person respond to aggression? What does this person consider to be aggression? How does this person change when under pressure?

All of this is essential information to know about a prospective staff member. Although this information is rarely a determining factor when I hire someone, it does give me insight into how I can provide effective leadership.

In addition, we have found it to be of great value to keep detailed profiles of all staff members available for other staff members to review at any time. This information becomes a valuable resource in avoiding potential conflict or solving emerging conflict. Because we place such a premium on communication and transparency, a potential staff member who is uncomfortable with this type of self-revelation would never be comfortable on my team. Our system is set up in such a way that a potential staff member can determine these issues before the process goes too far.

Another important value of the availability of behavioral profiles is that it allows a potential staff member to learn all he (or she) can about each of the current team members, especially the senior leader. I *want* this person to read my profile. I *want* to spend time talking with him. I *want* this person to ask me the tough questions. This is one example of how mentoring can begin even before a new person comes aboard.

I also encourage all new or potential team members to talk to other staff members in private. I urge them to ask the rest of the staff what it is like to work for me and to let them openly discuss what they like and don't like about working for me. I do not want any surprises for me or for a new staff member. Before someone joins my team I want us both to know all we can about one another.

The Current Crisis

Like modeling, mentoring is one of the lost arts of leadership. Leaders do not mentor because they were not mentored. Mentoring is not even in their leadership paradigm. In many cases, people are thrust into leadership positions by virtue of their degree or by a promotion and receive little or no training or preparation for the job. This forces them to try and learn how to lead on their own. By trial and error (and usually a great deal of error) they either fail or succeed. More often than not, they fail and are removed only to be replaced by someone else who is equally unprepared for the responsibility. Even worse is when a failed leader is maintained in the position because of seniority, tenure, office politics or family connections. This phenomenon is sometimes called the "Peter Principle," which says that in any organization people tend to rise to their level of incompetence and remain there.

Good leaders are developed more than they are discovered.

Mentoring is sorely needed today for the simple reason that good leaders are developed more than they are discovered. Because of the co-dependent nature of modern society, responsible people are scarce and effective leaders are even harder to find. This is true not only in the business world but also in the church. Since responsible, well-developed people are so scarce, we must develop them. It's not enough to simply address a person's job skills. No matter what our organization, success requires that we also give attention to the social, moral, emotional and spiritual development of people. If leadership is in their future, we must cultivate their leadership skills. Mentoring is a powerful tool in that process.

Society has changed. Our judicial system no longer holds people responsible for their actions. Students graduate from high school who cannot read because they are never held responsible. Unions and government regulations often make it impossible to enforce high work standards. The quality of the American workforce has been in continual decline for years. Government leaders attempt to buy votes by offering life with no responsibilities. Our country thrives on co-dependency. The entire world's system is one that nurtures co-dependency and irresponsibility.

For this reason every segment of society is suffering. Good employees are harder to find. The stable segment of society is shrinking year by year. Therefore, any organization that hopes to endure and succeed must be committed to developing people as never before. It wasn't many years ago when most people entering the workforce could reasonably be expected to possess a healthy work ethic and at least a modicum of basic job skills. Not so today. In our day, it is increasingly rare for people entering the workforce, either from college, graduate school or from the "street" to display highly-developed social or work skills. Many of those who do possess meaningful skills are so self-centered that they have no concept of team effort, personal ethics, morals and responsibility. Self-advancement seems to be their only concern.

American culture, which glorifies the individual, has become the accepted norm. There is no realization of synergy. Healthy nationalism is a foreign concept. It matters not how the group suffers as long as the individual is gratified. This is the age of self. Thus, there is little loyalty, commitment or integrity.

Churches, businesses and other organizations now find themselves in the position of having to teach not only job skills but also cultivate in people a work ethic, the value of commitment and other areas of personal responsibility. We can no longer assume that the people coming through our doors already possess these things. Traditional methods and assumptions are no longer valid because they are no longer in touch with current realities.

The church should be the one place where the bedrock values for life, success and leadership are cultivated. Like the early Sunday schools that taught people to read, the church can meet this desperate need in society. Rather than cursing the darkness, we can be the light that shows the way. Serving in the local church should be a development process that mentors and models unparalleled leadership. The church should be the place the world looks to for its great leaders and workers!

The Mentoring Process

For all these reasons it is vitally important that once you *do* find the right people, you invest in them. Like modeling, mentoring requires a big investment up front but pays off in much bigger dividends later on. As soon as a new employee or staff person comes through your door, you should start them through the process of orientation and training so they can flow with your company. Put the new team members, whether paid or volunteer, through an orientation and training program that prepares them to be personally developed. Many companies in recent years have invested in programs to address employee needs not directly related to the workplace, such as personal financial counseling services, crisis counseling services, on-site child care services and others.

Upon completing a general orientation and training program, a new team member is ready to be mentored. Mentoring can happen through one individual, but it is usually more effective to place a new member with a succession of mentors chosen because of their demonstrated knowledge and effectiveness in a given area. Such a sequential mentoring process affords the new team member the opportunity to observe each aspect of the job performed by an expert, ask questions and perform each job aspect under the watchful guidance and one-on-one feedback of that expert. In addition, the new team member can benefit from the insights, "tricks of the trade," time-saving but quality-enhancing shortcuts and techniques and wisdom that his or her mentor has acquired through personal experience—valuable assets that cannot be codified in a book or learned from a programmed training module.

This sequential mentoring process also should be progressive. As people learn how to use the skills that are needed at their current level of responsibility, their responsibilities should increase accordingly. The more they prove themselves to be responsible and trustworthy, the more responsibility and trust they should be given and the more their self-confidence and the amount and quality of their personal development will grow.

Years ago when we honestly evaluated our church and the programs we offered, we realized that what had once been very effective, was now no longer meeting the needs. In order to continue to be effective and develop effective leaders we had to rethink nearly every area of our ministry. After years of searching and experimenting, I finally found the key to developing the kind of leaders I wanted. For us, it involved fewer services with pulpit teaching and more development of people skills. We needed more opportunities to model servant ministry. We modified our small groups so people could process what they were learning. In short, we adopted a training and development process focused around modeling and mentoring.

We discovered that the same system that developed good disciples also would develop effective leaders. We no longer had one system for developing church members and another for developing leaders; it all happened at the same time. Promoting leaders was just a part of the continuum of developing disciples. Leadership is, after all, a deeper commitment to those character-istics that all people should exemplify on some level.

Now, when individuals first comes to our church, we seek to provide them with a sponsor who comes into their homes and shares some basic principles of being a believer. All of our sponsors are trained by experienced sponsors who take them out and model sponsoring a few times. Then they are observed while they sponsor. Once the sponsors are comfortable, then they are sent out with someone they will teach. Ideally, this approach should produce a never-ending cycle of converts, sponsor trainees and sponsors.

The sponsor helps motivate the new convert to attend church, answers his (or her) questions and basically becomes a support base for six weeks. If a deeper relationship develops dur-ing that time, that is fine. By this time the new convert will be developing friendships of his own choice. It is also at this time that the new convert is more in a relationship with the Small Group Leader. He has spent the previous six weeks attending a Small Group. In this small, comfortable setting, he has learned to open up and talk very freely. During the first six weeks, the spon-sor also encourages the new convert to participate in three very important functions:

1. *Members Class*, where he learns about the meaning of commitment and the specifics regarding finding a place to serve.

2. *Foundations of Faith Class*, where he learns the foundational teachings and doctrines of the Christian faith.

3. *Discovery Class*, where he is profiled to match his skills, gifts and passions to specific areas in the church where he might be prepared to serve.

As you can see, this entire progressive development process utilizes a combination of corporate (classroom) and individual mentoring. At no time in the process is the person who is being developed left alone to fend for himself. A mentor of some kind, whether his sponsor, his Small Group Leader, his group members or someone else is always available to answer questions, to model and to assist in any other way needed. If all has gone well, at the end of the process the person has progressed from new convert to a discipled, well-grounded believer ready to serve and potentially ready for development as a leader.

This is just an example of how a mentoring process can work in a church setting. Mentoring can be modified to be successfully implemented in churches of any size. The same is true with businesses or other organizations. Size does not matter. Mentoring can work in any business setting of any size and at any level. The key is for current leadership to believe in the value of mentoring as a leadership development process and to be *committed* to that process.

As far as value, mentoring is another ancient, time-honored, biblically based, proven approach to learning and development. Classroom teaching develops the mind but mentoring, centered as it is on one-to-one interaction, develops not only the mind but the heart and spirit also. Mentoring is only possible when combined with modeling; in fact, modeling is inherent in mentoring. In combination, modeling and mentoring comprise an unrivaled method for developing workers and leaders in any area and any discipline.

Notice too that I described mentoring as a leadership development *process*. That is very important. Mentoring will not happen until and unless current leadership in an organization *make* it happen. And the only way to do that is to develop a *process* for mentoring or, in other words, a *system*. Mentoring must be deliberate, planned, ongoing, systematic and designed in such a way as to become self-sustaining as mentors develop other mentors who in turn develop still others. This too is in keeping with another key to success: the law of multiplication.

Mentoring can work in any business setting of any size and at any level.

As important as mentoring is, however, we cannot let it cost us our vision. Mentoring must incorporate both personal and corporate goals. Remember, everyone must win! Mentoring is not the goal. It is the process. For this reason it is sometimes wise and even necessary, at least in the earliest stages of establishing the mentoring process, to bring in people from outside who are committed to helping us develop the people in our organization. Sometimes consultants have to come in to develop the current leaders. Once the "first generation" of leaders and/or mentors is developed and successfully generates the second generation, the entire process can then continue to grow from within.

Another precaution about mentoring is that we must avoid the tendency to give our time to people based solely on their potential. Otherwise we open ourselves up to experience the frustration of watching our investment go down the tubes when that person fails or quits. Potential alone should never be the basis for selecting a person to mentor. It is never a reliable indicator of what a person will do. In most cases, people will do what they have done in the past. Mentoring is not a right but a privilege that comes with trust, respect and responsibility. No one should be mentored who has not earned the privilege through proven trust and dependability.

Mentoring Is a Form of Nurturing

Many leaders abandon their personal development and place all their attention on helping others. Too often they deplete themselves and do not get needed support from their leader. In our current impersonal world, it seems that many senior leaders want to pass on intellectual instruction in a seminar and then retreat to the golf course. Too often we think that giving the information is enough. The truth is, all people, including leaders and potential leaders, need nurturing in order to grow, mature and maintain productivity. Mentoring is a form of nurturing.

Like many, I spent much of my life thinking that nurturing was just for the weak. I wanted strong people around me. I wanted those who could carry their load with little input from me. My warped paradigm prevented me from the very thing I desired: strong leaders. I failed to see that planting a leader is like planting a tree. If it is to become and stay strong, it must have nourishment. Although it is true that a leader should be a personal self-encourager, I still have a moral and ethical responsibility to minister to him or her.

As a "high achiever," I felt internal, self-imposed pressure to accomplish certain tasks. This unhealthy sense of responsibility made me feel that I was wasting my time if I spent too much time with staff members. After all, if I was with people I wasn't accomplishing tasks. I failed to realize one of the greatest laws of leadership: multiplication. Through the principle of multiplication, I have accepted the reality that I can accomplish much more through people than I can alone.

To accomplish anything through and with people we must be willing to have a slow start. As I said before, it is always slower to invest in others at the beginning. The value, however, of the delayed dividends far exceeds the investment. Through the law of multiplication, I accept the fact that a slow start that involves and develops others is a sure start. In the end, I have more time for personal accomplishments if I invest more quality time into those around me. If everyone around me is living their dream, I will certainly be a success.

This requires a deep sense of personal security. If I invest in others, they will have more personal accomplishments than I. They will do many of the things I desire to do. And worse, they will get the credit. A secure leader invests in others who accomplish more tasks than he or she does. Each person in the process accepts his or her role to accomplish the law of multiplication. In order to enter the multiplication phase we must surrender ego-driven leadership styles. Leaders invest in and lead others. If we are not investing in others, we are not leaders, just high achievers. A high achiever and a leader are not the same thing.

A high achiever and a leader are not the same thing.

One of my first hurdles was discovering the difference between encouragement and nurturing. I always thought nurturing was for the weak and encouragement was for the strong. But the opposite is true. Nurturing is for those who will allow themselves to be developed; encouragement is for those who have not yet committed to success. Nurturing is for those who are running the race; encouragement is for those who have not yet decided to run. You only fertilize (nurture) the seed after it is planted.

I found myself encouraging those who were already committed. I am sure they felt I was being superficial. It is sort of like the cheerleaders trying to get the team to score after the game is over and the team has won. On the other hand, I was giving a lot of personal time and attention attempting to nurture those who had not yet really decided they even wanted to play in the game. In the end, I would have had tremendous investment in them and they did not even show up for the game. I was burning myself out on those who had never made a commitment. I felt frustrated, and they felt pressured. The people who were working the plan felt unappreciated and ignored!

We must commit our nurturing (mentoring) to those who have shown themselves committed to the cause. We must not allow those who labor to languish while we give our greatest investment to those who are not sure what they want to do. Too often we neglect the ones we can help and give ourselves to those we cannot. We must follow the simple scriptural principle, *"Invest in good ground!"*

By mentoring people, we also develop mentors. Mentors become the influencers in the organization that makes it great. Their investment in others is multiplied beyond their wildest expectations. These mentors become the leadership team that takes the organization to true greatness.

Every company is looking for great leaders. They don't realize that most of their great leaders already work for them. They are the undeveloped people who need only to be developed. Mentoring creates an endless cycle of developing quality workers and leaders that fulfill the laws of multiplication.

Chapter Nine

MULTIPLICATION

❦

Modeling and mentoring are two aspects of leadership that are all but lost in today's church and corporate environments, yet they are absolutely crucial to the key factor in measuring true leadership success: *multiplication*. To state it plainly and simply, *effective leaders reproduce themselves through multiplication*. There is no other satisfactory indicator for the success of a leader.

Fulfilling a vision, making a specific mark on society and training leaders and workers all come down to one word...*multiplication*. Great leaders multiply themselves. A leader may have all the right skills, know all the right principles and even have a bang-up team working with him (or her), but if he is not committed to multiplying and is not working a plan that is geared for multiplying, he is not truly successful. He may have some great achievements from time to time, but nothing that will prove sustainable over the long run. Eventually, without multiplying leaders who then multiply other leaders, he will run out of steam and a breakdown will occur somewhere in the process, resulting in frustration and failure to reach goals.

Vision is the starting place. Vision is an imprint that should be made on every aspect of the organization. Every person should be functioning to make that imprint on everything he or she touches. The person standing at the cash register should be fulfilling the vision of the leader in the boardroom. The worker sweeping the parking lot should be making the imprint of the vision born in the pastor's prayer closet. It should happen because those people are living their dream. It should happen without control. But it must happen through a shared vision that has been birthed, cultivated and multiplied through every person from the front door to the back door!

Effective, successful leadership, as we saw in Chapter One, is a balance between accomplishing goals and developing people. A leader who focuses only on accomplishing goals is little more than a boss, a user of people to achieve personal ends. The mark of a true leader is the accomplishment of goals while at the same time developing people by freeing and helping them to pursue their own dreams as they pursue the goals of the organization. The leaders who emerge from this effort then become a part of raising up and releasing new leaders who will then repeat the same process with the people who work with them. This is the principle of multiplication.

Multiplication occurs when a particular number or object duplicates itself repeatedly. Responsible leaders realize that the way they work with people will cause a subtraction, an addition or a multiplication of themselves. No interaction is static; it either gives or takes away from the organization and its goals.

Negative interaction will result in friction, frustration, high stress levels, frequent turnover and an epidemic of people being blown out of any future effective service. Nobody can function well for very long in a prolonged negative environment. Unfortunately, many so-called leaders today have created and perpetuated just such an environment. Because of their own unawareness, they don't understand that they are the cause. And since they don't understand the cause, they don't know how to correct the problem. Usually they blame the workers. It's sort of like the gag sign that says, "Attention all employees: The beatings will continue until morale improves." Don't forget that continuing to do things the same way and expecting different results is one definition of insanity. If the current situation is not working, something needs to be changed. Usually it's the leadership paradigm.

All problems are leadership problems. I did not say they were the *fault* of leadership. Responsibility does not consider who should be blamed. Responsibility considers who can and should take action. Any ongoing problem is a leadership problem! Why? Only leadership has the abiding power to solve problems. No matter whose fault it is, leaders don't find the blame. They find solutions!

Positive interaction will result in either addition or multiplication, again depending on the current leadership paradigm. Everything grows by one of two means: addition or multiplication. Both require about the same amount of effort; it is simply a different kind of effort. Addition adds people who can do the job. This is the "hireling mentality"; you need more work done so you hire another worker. They may do the work, but that's *all* they will do. The *end* of addition is the task to be accomplished. As long as there are sufficient people to do the job, that's all that matters.

Multiplication, on the other hand, develops people not only to perform a task but also to understand *why* they are performing the task. Multiplication invests in the person, gives ownership and responsibility, develops the person's ability to act independently and takes the worker to a higher level of value in the organization. It also cultivates their potential leadership skills. Unlike addition, which ends with each task completed, multiplication is repeated time and time again. It is the duplication of self, the reinvestment of our skills *and* experience. Multiplication reproduces us in others, who then reproduce themselves in still others.

For years, technology visionaries have dreamed of self-sustaining machines that could repair themselves and reproduce themselves. Much of current interest is focused on the potential of nanotechnology with microscopic machines that could not only replicate themselves endlessly, but also, theoretically, build anything of any size or complexity that the machine's programmers desire. This illustrates how multiplication can work. The big difference is that in life we are dealing with people, not machines. Any successful leadership paradigm must be committed to multiplication. Don't mistake this for the duplication of clones who simply copy the task. This is the development of responsible people in a way that values and enhances their dignity and worth.

The leader who grows by addition has to train every person who comes on board. He (or she) has to be present for every transaction. In contrast, the leader who grows by multiplication replaces himself by the investment he makes in others. By making others successful, the one who leads by multiplication is pushed to higher levels of success by the very people he leads to success. It is the ultimate win-win situation.

Under multiplying leadership, the sky truly is the limit because people are developed and released to visualize their dreams. Once they can visualize their dreams, they can set their goals, set their intention on those goals and make it happen.

The Power of Multiplication

Multiplication happens to the degree that we invest in people. Great leaders develop the people while accomplishing the goals. They recognize that people are our greatest resources. More than this, they also recognize that merely accomplishing the goal will result in micro-management with their presence required to accomplish every task. If, on the other hand, they develop the *person* in the *process* of accomplishing the goal, they free themselves. The wise leader knows that multiplication is the *only* way to experience personal freedom from the frustration of micro-management.

Addition has a deceitful allure. It is quicker and easier in the beginning and actually makes it appear to get us to our goals faster. And it will...in the short term. But every minute we spend in addition, we push our long-term goals farther from us. Addition creates robots that can repeat a task. The moment there is the need for decision-making or independent thinking, however, it all turns to frustration. That's when you hear the desperate cry of the frustrated leader, "They can't do anything without me."

Teach people how to do and why to do and you are on your way to multiplication. Give them the proper training and the power to act and they will act. Help them understand and define the scope of their responsibility. Give them freedom through responsibility and you will have freedom.

Multiplication, when it begins to pay off, puts everything on a fast track.

Multiplication starts slowly. In the beginning, it takes far more time and requires a much larger investment, but eventually it hits the exponential curve where it produces growth beyond our wildest imagination. And incredibly, that growth continues to reflect our original values and intentions. Multiplication, when it begins to pay off, puts everything on a fast track.

Over time, multiplication will require *less* personal involvement from the leader, yet will bring no decrease in quality. In fact, quality will actually *increase* dramatically! I have found that my team makes everything I do better. Because I am surrounded by people who are willing to think, encouraged to think and required to think, every person I involve in a project brings it to a new level of quality and effectiveness.

It is impossible to underestimate the power of the principle of multiplication. We can see a powerful illustration of this in the legend of the invention of chess. According to the legend, the emperor of India informed his subjects that he wanted a new game invented and would reward the inventor of the best one. An old man came to the emperor with chess. After looking over all the other inventions and seeing chess demonstrated, the emperor declared chess the winning invention. He was so impressed and excited by the new game, in fact, that he offered the inventor anything in his kingdom.

After thinking for a few moments, the inventor said, "All I wish, your majesty, is one grain of rice."

The emperor was astonished. "Just one grain of rice?"

"Yes. Just one grain of rice on the first square of the chess board, two grains on the second square, four grains on the third square, and so on, with each square of the board receiving twice the number of grains as the square before it."

That may not sound like much of a prize until you do the math. A chess board has 64 squares. Had the emperor attempted to fulfill the inventor's request he would have gone bankrupt because 2 to the 64th power would equal 18 million billion grains of rice! At 10 grains of rice per square inch of rice fields, this would mean that the entire surface of the earth would have to be covered with rice fields twice over, oceans included. Long before then, even before reaching the halfway point—the 32nd square— all the rice in India would have been depleted. In contrast, using the principle of addition and placing on each square one more grain of rice than on the previous square (one on the 1st, two on the 2nd, three on the 3rd, four on the 4th and so forth through all 64 squares) would yield a total of only 2080 grains of rice!

Such is the power of multiplication!

Here's another illustration. As a pastor committed to winning people to Christ, I did an equation once and discovered that if 50 people each won 2 people to Christ per year and then each of *those* won 2 people a year and each of *those* won 2 people, and so on, in ten years' time the entire population of Huntsville, Alabama, would be won to Christ. At the same rate, in less than 20 years, the entire population of the United States would be won and, within our lifetime, the population of the entire world.

Such is the power of multiplication!

The First Law of Multiplication

Multiplication is all about duplication. In order to multiply I must reproduce myself. However, multiplication is not the mere duplication of a specific task. It is also the reproduction of values and philosophies. Multiplication is about the person as much as it is about the goal. People not only learn to do the work, but they also learn why it is done in a certain way. This is the *secret* to multiplication.

Breakdown in the workplace can occur for several reasons. The most common cause of breakdown is when people do not perform their job as they should and the second is when people make decisions that are inconsistent with the overall goals of the organization. Both of these situations normally result from people knowing a task but not knowing the "why"; knowing the job but not knowing the philosophies that lie behind it.

When seeking to become multiplying leaders, it is very important to learn the *first law of multiplication: followers will do it like we do—plus or minus a little*.

In other words, if we leave *anything* out, they will leave out a lot. If we omit any part of the process, we are saying that none of it is important. It's like telling the people, "Take your choice." If we skip a step, they'll skip ten steps. If we add things that seem to violate the plan—things they don't understand—they will add. Every time they have a problem, they will not go back to the blueprint; they will simply add another step until it no longer has any similarity to the goal. If we tell but don't show (model), they won't even tell. Our plan to multiply leaders can break down with the first generation if we deviate.

It's really easy to make a mistake here. I see it happen all the time, and it's happened to me more times than I care to count. Anytime I have gotten in trouble with a staff member or someone else over this it is because I treated that person like the *exception* to the rule, skipping over some part of the process because I *assumed* he or she already knew it. Knowing something and seeing it modeled are two different things. Whenever we assume we can skip part of the process with someone we are training, a breakdown in the multiplication process is inevitable. Even if the person we are training *does* already grasp the part we skip over, that person will very likely assume that anyone he or she trains will grasp it as well and will skip over that part of the training. That assumption may very likely be incorrect, and if so breakdown will occur.

There's a big difference between multiplying and hiring.

Multiplication occurs when the same goals and values are duplicated. If we are not taking our people through a clearly defined process of teaching, modeling, mentoring with a lot of discussion and interaction, even if they see what we do, they won't understand *why* we do it. They won't understand what we value. Even if they duplicate our methods for a while, if they don't understand what we value, eventually there will be a breakdown.

Developing an environment for multiplication has a lot to do with attitude. There's a big difference between multiplying and hiring. Let's consider a few contrasts. If you are a multiplier, you are a *leader*. You are modeling and mentoring and going before people. If all you are doing is hiring, you're a *boss*. You know what a boss does? A boss tells people to do things he doesn't want to do, doesn't like to do and is unwilling to do. A boss says, "Do this." A leader says, "Let me show how this is done." A boss won't bother to tell you the process (if the boss even has one). A leader will walk you through the process. A boss says, "It doesn't matter why." A leader says, "Let's make sure you know why!"

If you are a multiplier, you have a *recruit*; if you are only hiring, you have a *hireling*. A recruit is interested in more than just the job; he wants to learn everything he can about the philosophies and values as well. A hireling is interested only in what he was hired to do—and nothing more. A multiplying environment has people with *purpose* who are committed to *growth* while a hireling environment has employees who are committed only to a paycheck.

A hireling mentality will break down the process of multiplication. Usually we think of a hireling as a person hired for a job who works only for the money. Sometimes, however, the hireling may be a leader who has a hireling mentality. A situation arises and this leader says, "I've got to hire somebody—quick!" The person he hires will do the job (hopefully), but when that person has done all he (or she) can do, he will want the leader to hire somebody else. Why? Because *a hireling never multiplies. Never.*

If we want to be successful, multiplying leaders, we have to eradicate from our thinking any hint of a hireling mentality and view every person not as just a worker to do a job but as a person of skill and value and a potential leader-in-the-making.

These same principles apply to a non-paid team member. There are those who have the volunteer attitude and there are those who have the non-paid staff attitude. If you are non-paid staff with a servant's heart, you can flow with the multiplication process. In fact, this is the best way to develop future paid staff. If you only see yourself as a volunteer, you too may have the "hireling" mentality. The difference between a servant and a volunteer is enormous. A servant is not easily offended because his focus is always on the goals of the team. Non-paid staff hold the same values and standards as the paid staff. Volunteers give the standard they are willing to give. They tend to set their own standards instead of accept the standard of the organization. If a non-paid staff is informed that the work is not up to standard, his or her commitment to the goals and vision causes him or her to bring the work up to standard. A volunteer will say, "You mean I did all that work for nothing? I'm just not appreciated!"

We avoid the use of the terminology "volunteer" because we want everyone to know that his or her job is important. Everyone is equally valuable to the goal. Everyone is held to the same standard of quality and responsibility. Everyone has to take ownership!

Multiplication Requires Systems

True multiplication requires systems. In fact, multiplication cannot occur without systems. Each team member, whether paid or non-paid, whether management or worker, must pass through a systematic development that moves from philosophy to procedure. Multiplication requires not only that we have a system, but also that we must work that system.

Of all the weaknesses I have seen in people I try to develop, perhaps the greatest is a lack of value for working systems. Nothing is more disheartening than to develop a great system that you know works, put it in people's hands and watch them fail because they didn't use it. If someone is unfamiliar with working systems or has never succeeded in something like this before, he is liable to look at the system and say, "Oh, I don't need to do that," and mark it off. "Hmm, I'm not comfortable with that one," and he marks that one off too. "I don't feel up to this one either," and he marks it off. A few months down the line his team is falling apart and he's complaining that nobody wants to work on his team. The truth is, he didn't know what it took to succeed and didn't trust the system he was given to bring success.

The inexperienced see the system as a roadblock. The experienced see it as a road map. It makes one feel confined and another feel free. Teaching people to work systems not only ensures their success in our organizational endeavors, but it also develops their professional skills and helps them succeed at other jobs. Many of our non-paid team members are excelling in their jobs because of what they learn in our development programs.

People who can be taught and *shown* the value of working a system will discover that one of the greatest single obstacles to their success and the fulfillment of their dreams has been removed. When people work together on a team or in an organization, pursue a common goal and follow a proven system, success is virtually guaranteed. What's more, when that system develops people along the way, they discover that they can apply the same approach and methods to every area of their lives and succeed in whatever personal goals and dreams they set for themselves. A system helps ensure that everybody wins—the organization because it accomplishes its goals, and the people in the organization because they grow, add quality to their lives and learn how to turn their dreams into reality.

There are certain specific elements that any successful system must have. As an example, I want to share with you a brief overview of the process we use at Impact to develop what we call a "dream team."[1] These same elements, or something very similar, should be a part of any system, whether in a church or corporate setting.

Multiplication cannot occur without systems.

The *Mission Statement* is a summary that describes the aims, values and overall plan of an organization or an individual. It concisely expresses clearly identified goals. It answers the question, "Why do we exist?"

The *Vision Statement* provides a quantitative description of the successful fulfillment of the goal. In other words, it describes what success will look like. You have to know what your target looks like before you can shoot at it.

The *Fulfillment Statement* explains what we will do to accomplish the goal, how we will fulfill the Mission Statement. This is sometimes the place where we express what we will do that is unique to fulfill the goals.

Philosophy of Ministry. This expresses the philosophical values that will be observed while pursuing the goal, how we will think toward and treat the people in the organization as well as the people we serve.

The *Emotional Impact Statement* explains how we will make people feel in the process. This may be the most important element of all. Without it none of the other system components will work. The Emotional Impact Statement helps us answer the questions, "What is the emotional impact we want to have on the people our team is serving?" "How do we want people to feel?"

We can *do* the right system and still have the wrong impact unless we are governed by the knowledge of how we want people to feel. The truth can stop being true if the way it is delivered does not accomplish the intended goal. How do we want people to feel? That's the crucial question.

Meet My Team. This element explains who it will take and what skills will be required to reach the goal.

The Character Sketch describes the character expected on the team in order to ensure success. Every area requires different kinds of character aspects, but one thing is certain: People of low character have no business serving on a team. It doesn't matter if they have all the right skills or more talent than anyone else, if they have a character problem and you put them on your team, you're asking for trouble.

In a church setting, we want to develop people. We do not reject them personally because of character issues. Church is not a celebration of the perfect. It is the developing (discipling) of those who have answered the call to follow Christ. Don't ignore them and don't reject them. Try to find some other way for them to serve while you or someone else seeks to help them build their character. But don't put them on your team until they have the character for the job.

The Training Plan tells what we will do to equip our team. It lays out the introductory and ongoing training required of every team member.

The Budget provides the cost and financial goals. It tells how much it will cost to reach our goals and achieve success.

Policies and Procedures provides us the guidelines and the management policies that will guide the work of the team or the organization. It gets down to the nuts and bolts of what it will take to reach our goals.

Every worker and every leader must be completely knowledgeable and fully committed to the plan. Every year all of our workers and leaders repeat the Dream Team training for their department. It always brings them back to the fundamentals of our existence and function. It renews their awareness and commitment to our systems.

Multiplication can occur only when a clear-cut system is in place and is used consistently. Systems are simply the way you do things every time. A systematic approach to training, mentoring and modeling is the only way to get systematic results. Systems ensure true multiplication, the duplication of skills within a workplace philosophy and provide trainees with assurances, clear-cut goals and a fair opportunity.[2] Systems ensure that procedures that must be exact are done so, giving room for creativity and freedom in the areas that allow variety and innovation.

Systems Are Proactive

We all have two choices in life: We can either be *proactive* or we can be *reactive*. If you are a reactive person, whether as a spouse, a worker or a leader, you are out of control because your next decision is going to be made by your next encounter. If you do not have a system to fall back on and define what you do, your next encounter will force you into a reaction. Proactive people make decisions in advance so they don't have to make decisions under pressure. That's why a system is so important. Systems are proactive by nature. If you are building or working a system, you are already being proactive.

Proactive behavior has several important characteristics. First, proactive behavior is focused on a destination. If you are proactive, you have already decided where you want to go. Second, proactive behavior is positive. In other words, a proactive person is always looking at the "why" for doing something rather than the "why not." He is always looking for ways to get the job done rather than coming up with reasons why it can't be done.

In addition, proactive behavior is "toward" behavior, not "away from" behavior. What's the difference? People motivated by "away from" behavior are always trying to avoid pain while "toward" people are motivated *toward* goals and destinations. Don't get me wrong; "away from" behavior has its value. If you walk outside and find a huge dog snarling and growling at you and foaming at the mouth, you'd better run "away from" it. "Away from" behavior is a defense mechanism and is important in its place. For some people, unfortunately, "away from" behavior is their primary way of reacting to life.

If you are building or working a system, you are being proactive.

You can't go very far in life with "away from" behavior because it is reactionary in nature. This means that whenever you encounter something threatening, you move away from it. Your life becomes like the ball in a pinball game, bouncing from one encounter to another with no control or destination.

Proactive people, however, are "toward" people because they keep moving toward the goal despite obstacles, setbacks or even pain. Their passion for the goal and for success outweighs the discomfort they must sometimes endure getting there. A good system, however, minimizes discomfort and maximizes satisfaction on the way to the goal.

Because proactive behavior is "toward" behavior, it is initiated by the *purpose*, not the problem. Reactive behavior is initiated by the problem, not the purpose. Hence, it is always in problem-solving mode—"crisis management." Although it is true we must solve problems, solving problems and moving toward a goal are not the same thing. Proactive systems thinkers solve problems by moving people toward the goal. They get them back on the track. Reactive people seem to lack a basic understanding or belief in systems. When a crisis arises, they have no systematic, predetermined way to deal with it. In the heat of the moment, they "shoot from the hip" and usually miss.

By its very nature, then, proactive behavior is *preventive*, not corrective. The goal of proactive leaders is to prevent problems before they happen rather than deal with them after they happen. Systems help in this because they spell out in detail the way things are to be done, including contingencies: "If this happens, do this." Murphy's Law says that anything that *can* go wrong *will* go wrong. On the surface that sounds like a cynical and even pessimistic statement, but it carries an important principle for systems. People in high-reliability fields such as the space program assume this as a bedrock principle in designing and building their systems. Their proactive thinking challenges them to foresee any possible error, mistake or problem that could possibly occur and to design contingency plans. If you plan your system around the assumption that anything that can go wrong will go wrong, you will be proactive in predicting the problems you and your people are likely to encounter and can plan ahead to deal with any contingency. Prevention is always easier and cheaper than correction.

One of the greatest values for proactive systems is emotional. When we have a system in place, we are not burdened with thinking every situation through in the emotions of the moment. That alone is an incredible relief to the leader. When we say "no" to a worker and refer him or her to the system we must follow, it does not feel like we are saying "no" to the individual personally. In fact, I almost never say no to anyone. When people say they want to do something, I simply tell them the procedure for doing it. If they can make it through the process, they must be qualified. If not, the choice to quit is theirs, not mine.

The Law of Heart Physics®

The Second Law of Thermodynamics says that any matter in the universe left to itself tends toward chaos. This is true of human behavior also. If we are not committed to deliberate proactive behavior, then we are always moving toward chaos in our lives. We have to get up every morning and decide whether we're going to have a good day or a bad day. Certainly, we can't control what happens to us during the day, but we can control how we respond to it. We can be proactive or reactive.

We have to approach every situation with an intention of whether we want it to go well or go badly. Some people by their continually reactive behavior set themselves up for constant crises, disasters and failures. If we don't have a deliberate intention for something to go well, it will move toward chaos. And even if it does go well, it won't go as well as it could have.

These same laws of physics that rule our material world are reflected in the function of man's heart. This is what I call the "Heart Physics®": where there is not proactive behavior, there is chaos. Reactive behavior waits until there is a problem—which is usually too late. Proactive behavior anticipates the problem and prevents it.

Reactive behavior is initiated by an outside source. Proactive behavior is stimulated from an inside source. Proactive behavior puts me in control of the destination. Reactive behavior puts others in control of the destination. Systems prevent the law of chaos from flourishing.

The Four Laws of Proactive Behavior

Let's break this down a little further and look at the four laws of proactive behavior.

The first law of proactive behavior says, "I will act *before* there is a problem." Suppose you are getting ready to do something you've never done before. How are you going to figure it out? How are you going to anticipate problems in an area that is new to you? One way is to close your eyes and think everything through. Envision yourself in that situation. Take yourself mentally through every step as if you were already doing it and you will suddenly realize parts you were not aware of before. By doing this dry run in your imagination you will discover all the missing pieces, all the things you didn't know and that you need to pass along to your people.

Another and perhaps better way is to brainstorm with other behavior types so that you get input that allows you to see the whole thing from every side. Brainstorm with people who are different from you and who think differently because they will come up with insights from their particular perspective that you would never think of.

And of course, there is the wisdom of Proverbs that tells us to seek wise counsel. Find people who have done what you want to do. Almost anything you are trying to do, someone else has already done, at least in part. Through reading one book or listening to one audio program you could takes years of their life's success into your endeavor.

It's hard to do the wrong thing when our intention is to benefit someone.

The second law of proactive behavior says, "When there is no rule, I will act in accordance with the goals and philosophies of the team." A person who will not act when he (or she) doesn't know what to do is more concerned about how he looks than he is about what happens. Nobody wants to look stupid. But what's worse than looking stupid? Looking like you don't care.

People whose leaders take them through the process feel safe asking questions. They understand the goals and values of the team. When there is no rule to tell them what to do in an unexpected situation, they will be clear enough about the objectives to say, "Well, this will accomplish that." A basic rule of thumb is that if we walk in love we will almost always do the right thing where relating to people is concerned. It's hard to do the wrong thing when our intention is to benefit someone.

People who understand why they do what they do are far more apt to come up with the proper solution in the absence of a clear-cut procedure. They have a logic guiding their thought processes that can often lead them to the best solutions.

The third law of proactive behavior says that proactive people are driven by the values and goals of the team. They are not concerned with building or preserving their ego or advancing themselves at the expense of others. At all times they keep the goals and values of the team in front of them, and those goals and values guide everything they do.

Finally, the fourth law of proactive behavior says, "I will act without being told." Our purpose as leaders is not to create robots or clones. We are trying to create disciples—whole, well-developed, well-adjusted and confident people. We are trying to develop people who are not afraid to take risks to go after their dreams and become the people they truly want to be.

Growth, development and risks always involve a certain amount of failure before success is achieved. As leaders, we want people to know that failing is *safe*. I'd rather have people try, fail and learn from their failure, and try again, than for them to do nothing because they didn't know what to do. After all, the only difference between a successful person and a failure is that the successful person picked him or herself up one time more often than he or she fell and tried again.

In the end, multiplication is the only means to massive productivity, sustained quality, continual growth and a peaceful workplace. Multiplication leads to duplication. When true multiplication occurs, every person you develop will develop others. As the senior leader is freed from the arduous role of micro-manager, he or she is free to take the organization to new heights of success and profitability. While the daily work is being done without your constant involvement, you will find the freedom to pursue your ultimate dreams—and so will your people.

Endnotes

1. James B. Richards, *Developing Your Dream Team* (Huntsville, Alabama: Impact International Publications).

2. For more information about training with systems, see James B. Richards, *Ultimate Leadership* (Huntsville, Alabama: Impact International Publications).

Chapter Ten

THE POWER OF A
SHARED VISION

❦

It all began with a vision.

Who would ever have imagined that two brothers, bicycle mechanics from Dayton, Ohio, would fulfill the universal dream of man throughout the ages and change forever the future of transportation? Yet Wilbur and Orville Wright had a shared vision of conquering the problems and challenges of aerodynamics and making controlled, powered flight a reality.

They built their first glider in 1899. Beginning in 1900 they chose Kitty Hawk as their testing ground, a windy, sandy spot on the northern part of the Outer Banks of North Carolina. Because of its strong and almost constant wind, Kitty Hawk was the perfect place for the brothers to test their designs. Systematically they pursued their vision, making plans, designing, building and flying their own gliders, solving problems that arose and adjusting their designs or techniques in light of those problems and solutions. They learned both from their successes (flights) as well as from their failures (crashes).

The knowledge they gained from their glider flights and experiments proved invaluable as their designs for a powered aircraft evolved. One particular difficulty had stumped all pioneering aviators up to this point: straight-line flying or gliding was one thing; turning in mid-air while maintaining control was another. Through their constant experimenting and tinkering and adjusting and careful note-taking and observation, Wilbur and Orville finally hit on the solution. They discovered the concept of wing-warping. By physically warping the shape of the wing through controls manipulated by the pilot, they could execute controlled turns in mid-air.

Finally, on December 17, 1903, using an aircraft, a propeller and a powerful four-cylinder engine, all of their own design, Wilbur and Orville Wright made history. Orville flew their new airplane in controlled flight for 12 seconds and a distance of 120 feet. Later the same day, Wilbur flew the craft and stayed in the air for 59 seconds, covering 852 feet. Controlled, powered flight was now a reality, and the world would never be the same. In the words of poet and pilot John Magee, man had "slipped the surly bonds of earth and danced the skies on laughter-silvered wings."

Not bad for two brothers who never even finished high school! They visualized their dream, established their goals, set their intention—and made it happen.

It all began with a vision.

Speaking to a joint session of Congress on May 25, 1961, President John F. Kennedy said, "I believe that this nation should commit itself to achieving the goal, before this decade is out, of landing a man on the moon and returning him safely to the earth." President Kennedy did not invent this vision. He did not even live to see it achieved. He was not the originator, but he was the leader who ignited the fire of passion in our nation that saw it done.

The next eight years witnessed an incredibly synchronized effort of scientists, engineers, physicians, pilots, technicians and others that culminated on July 20, 1969, with astronaut Neil Armstrong's immortal words at the foot of the lunar module at Tranquility Base on the surface of the moon: "That's one small step for man; one giant leap for mankind."

Apollo 11 was the result of a shared vision where our nation in general and the aerospace industry in particular established goals, set the intention and made it happen.

It all began with a vision.

On August 28, 1963, Dr. Martin Luther King, Jr., speaking from the steps of the Lincoln Memorial to a massive crowd of demonstrators, said this:

> I have a dream that one day this nation will rise up and live out the true meaning of its creed: "We hold these truths to be self-evident: that all men are created equal"...I have a dream that my four little children will one day live in a nation where they will not be judged by the color of their skin but by the content of their character.

Dr. King did not originate the vision of civil rights and equality for all, but he gave shape and passion to that vision. His speech mobilized supporters of desegregation and prompted the passage of the Civil Rights Act of 1964. Inspired by his leadership, millions of Americans, blacks and whites alike, joined in a shared vision, established their goals, set their intention and changed the entire climate of American society.

It all began with a vision.

Jesus Christ told His disciples,

> *Go therefore and make disciples of all the nations, baptizing them in the name of the Father and of the Son and of the Holy Ghost, teaching them to observe all things that I have commanded you...* (Matthew 28:19-20).

and,

But you shall receive power when the Holy Spirit has come upon you; and you shall be witnesses to Me in Jerusalem, and in all Judea and Samaria, and to the end of the earth (Acts 1:8).

Fired by their shared vision and in obedience to the command of their Lord, Jesus disciples' proceeded to carry His vision and His message to all corners of the Roman Empire. Within three or four centuries, Christianity had thoroughly transformed the Roman Empire and was even expanding into other parts of the world. For 2,000 years, the followers of Jesus have continued to pursue His vision, carrying it into all parts of the world. In the process they have thoroughly transformed western culture, even though many in that culture today do not recognize the debt they owe to Christ and His church.

There is great power in a shared vision. Virtually nothing is impossible for those who share a common vision, pursue a common goal, set a common intention and go after it. *If you can dream it, you can do it!*

Building an Orchestra

Effective leadership means building winning teams and multiplying leaders. Good leaders have the ability to ignite in their people a passion for the shared vision of the organization while at the same time awakening in them the boldness and confidence to pursue their own personal vision and live their own personal dreams. When people are developed through teams by effective leaders, they also become aware of their personal potential as never before. This inspires them to pursue and fulfill their potential and to live the life they've always dreamed of.

Building a winning team is like building a good orchestra. An orchestra is, in fact, a team. The conductor is the leader because he is the one who brings everything together and enables everyone on the team to play in harmony. Like any good leader, the conductor cannot do everything needed on the team. He cannot play all the instruments. He may be a violinist but cannot play the trumpet. And even as a violinist, he likely has other violinists in the orchestra who are better than he is. This is as it should be. The conductor's skill lies not in being able to play everything well but in bringing together all those artists, many of whom are better than he is in what they do, and drawing out of them their very best.

Effective leadership means building winning teams and multiplying leaders.

As with any team, an orchestra requires many different skills to succeed. For example, there is the string section—violins, violas, cellos and basses—the backbone of any orchestra. The strings generally bear the brunt of the load in anything the orchestra performs, which is one reason why the string section is usually the largest section of the orchestra. Then there are the woodwinds, the flutes, clarinets, oboes and bassoons whose voices offer a completely different timbre from the strings. Playing the wind instruments also requires different skills than playing strings. The oboes and bassoons, with their reedy, nasally double-reed sound, can cut easily through the sounds of the rest of the orchestra, which is why usually only one or two of each are needed.

The brass instruments—trumpets, trombones, French horns and tubas—and the percussion section round out the orchestra. Each section and each instrument requires different skills, but each skill is equally important if the orchestra is to fulfill its vision—to create beautiful music. Unless every instrument is playing its part, the orchestra is incomplete. Unless every team member is present and playing his or her role, the final result is less than it could be and should be.

Any orchestra needs a plan (a system) if it hopes to succeed. Players don't come in and play just anything they want anytime they want in any key or tempo they want. There must be a plan to bring them into synchronicity—perfect harmony of vision, spirit, purpose and direction. The musical score is that plan and the conductor (leader) is the one who guides the team into following the plan and bringing their music to life. Like any good system, the score tells the orchestra (team) members exactly what they are supposed to do and when: which notes to play and in what key. The conductor sets the tempo and the mood of the piece through his (or her) interpretation of dynamics and the desires of the composer.

As the leader, the conductor brings everything together. The orchestra as a whole shares a common vision. Everybody in the group wants to make beautiful music, and each individual person wants to make the best personal contribution he or she can. Working together on the common vision of beautiful music works to everybody's benefit corporately and individually. By achieving their individual goals of being great at their instruments and fully committing to the goal of the orchestra, the team succeeds and each individual member has the personal satisfaction of a job well done. The individuals win and the team wins. As orchestra members play together in harmony, their own skills also improve. Everyone benefits. Through the corporate and individual fulfillment of goals and dreams the listener benefits through the beautiful music of many different instruments working together to perform a harmonic masterpiece.

Success breeds success. The more individual team members experience success, the more encouraged, strengthened and confident they become in pursuing their own goals. They start to think, *If I can succeed when I work with this team, then I should be able to succeed in my career and with my family and with my finances.* They begin to see possibilities they've never seen before. They start to understand how doing new things that draw them out of their comfort zones stretch and mature them to give them new confidence. They begin to realize the dreams they've had for years can become more than just dreams. Now they know how to pursue them in a way to make them come true.

Where Do You Want to Go?

In Chapter Four I asked the question, "Where do you want to go?" That is a personal question as well as a corporate question. As a leader you need to know where you want to take your team and your organization, but as a person you also need to know where you want to go in life. In life as in leadership, the sky is the limit. It all depends on how big your vision is and how willing you are to establish a plan—a system—and work that system. If you are willing to do whatever it takes, then your success is virtually assured.

Whether on a team, in a marriage or in any other area of life, if you can *dream* it, you can *do* it.

Visualize your dream. Where do you want to go? Get a clear picture in your mind of your destination.

Establish your goals. What will you need to do to get there? What skills or resources will it require?

Set your intention. Commit yourself to the goal without reservation.

Make a plan. Decide how you are going to get there. Develop your system—your plan for getting you to your destination. Goals are no good without a plan for meeting them. Be as specific as you can. Anticipate hazards, roadblocks and obstacles and plan how to get around them. Be ready to adjust the plan—often!

Launch out. Once your dream is clear, your goals in place, your plan is clear and your intention set, launch out and go for it! *Work your system!* If you have developed it well, it will take you where you want to go. If you see your dream, it can happen. If you *set your intention*, you summon the inner-resources to make it possible. If you are *flexible and adaptable*, you will find the way. If you fully *trust God*, you have unlimited resources. *If you do not quit… you cannot fail!*

Who Are You Going to Take With You?

Effective leaders multiply leaders. Good leaders are servants who duplicate themselves through modeling and mentoring, knowing that their success comes as they help others succeed. The heart desire of a servant is to assist others to do well and achieve their dreams. The heart desire of a leader is to accomplish the goal. As servant-leaders building teams we can succeed and help our churches, businesses and other organizations succeed by developing people into leaders, who develop other people into leaders who develop still other people into leaders. The greatest success is achieved by those teams and organizations that are equally committed to the goals of the organization and to the personal development of people.

True success never occurs at the expense of other people.

The final question is, "Who are you going to take with you?" Despite what many people in our society might believe, no one succeeds alone. And *true* success never occurs at the expense of other people. Personal success comes only to the degree that we are willing to bring others along with us, allowing them to share in the vision, the ownership and the success. When our corporate dream is fulfilled, every person who contributed will say, "It was my dream! I am a success." Every person will experience the thrill of victory.

The *lost art of leadership* is not realized through a set of complicated theories and endless details. It is not found in extreme force. Its strength is not found in high and lofty ideals that linger beyond the reach of mortal man. It is rediscovered daily by those men and women who have laid their ego down, who have the courage and character to return to the simple biblical concept of treating others as they themselves want to be treated, by upholding the ethical and moral principles upon which any good society has been built, by giving instead of taking, by following the model of the greatest leaders who ever lived!

It was, after all, Jesus, the greatest leader who has ever lived, who uttered immortal words about the nature of true leadership to a group of men who at the time struggled with their egos, vied for power and misunderstood and misrepresented most of His teachings. But their influence on the entire world indicates they must have gotten the message when He said, "If you want to be the greatest of all, be servant of all."

The greatness for leadership is in you, for surely you have the capacity to serve! Yield to that spiritual, ethical and moral voice in your heart and you will discover the *lost art of leadership* and you will live your dreams!

ABOUT THE AUTHOR

⋖⋗∞⋖⋗

D r. James B. Richards is the best-selling author of more than 15 books, including *How to Stop the Pain* and *Breaking the Cycle*. He is best described in one word: *pioneer*. Since 1972 he has proclaimed a message that is practical, relevant, simple, safe, and empowering. Through his personal, innovative, and sometimes outrageous ministry style, millions of people around the world have been drawn into a loving relationship with God while finding love and restoration in their personal relationships.

A best-selling author and successful teacher, theologian, and businessman, Dr. Richards is in high demand as a speaker and personal advisor to business people, clergy, and political leaders. His personal process of emerging from years of pain, dysfunction, and deep bitterness has given him proven tools for success in life, ministry, and business. Although he holds degrees in theology, human behavior, and medicine, his teaching is simple, well-rounded, understandable, and easy to apply. The results have been proven in nearly 30 years of personal, professional, and clinical application.

Dr. Richards is also the Senior Pastor of Impact of Huntsville. IOH is a local church that has been built by reaching beyond the boundaries of the church to those who do not know Jesus. Through innovative outreach, interactive multimedia presentation of the Gospel, and an uncanny ability to connect with the lost, hundreds of people come to Jesus in services at Impact of Huntsville every year.

Today Dr. James B. Richards is still living out of that same passion that took him to the streets over 30 years ago. His message to the church is simple: "When the world sees God in the church, they will fill our auditoriums and want to know God."

Books by
Dr. James B. Richards

*Becoming the Person You Want to Be: Discovering
Your Dignity and Worth*

Breaking the Cycle

Escape from Codependent Christianity

How to Stop the Pain

We Still Kiss

Taking the Limits Off God

The Gospel of Peace

The Prayer Organizer

Supernatural Ministry

Grace: The Power to Change

Leadership That Builds People, Volume 1

Leadership That Builds People, Volume 2

Effective Small Group Ministry

*My Church, My Family: How to Have a
Healthy Relationship with the Church*

Satan Unmasked: The Truth Behind the Lie